COLLECTING
AGATES AND
JASPERS
OF NORTH AMERICA

PATTI POLK

Krause Publications
An imprint of Penguin Random House LLC
penguinrandomhouse.com

Printed in China
7 9 10 8

ISBN 978-1-4402-3745-4

Cover Design by Sharon Bartsch
Designed by Sandi Carpenter
Edited by Kristine Manty and Caitlin Spaulding

Contents

Acknowledgments 4

Introduction to the Agates and Jaspers of North America 5

History, Folklore and Use of Agates and Jaspers 9

    Folklore 14

    Lapidary Uses 15

    Information on the Properties of Agates and Jaspers 17

    Agate and Jasper Terminology 20

    Commonly Found Patterns Occurring in Agate and Jasper 20

    Physical Forms of Agate and Jasper 22

    Common and Unusual Characteristics 23

Collecting Agates and Jaspers of North America 24

Agates and Jaspers of the U.S., Canada and Mexico 30

U.S., A-Z State Listings 33

Canada 233

    Alberta 236

    British Columbia 236

    Manitoba 240

    Nova Scotia 241

    Ontario 246

    Quebec 247

Mexico 248

    Chihuahua 251

    Coahuila 262

    Durango 263

    Nayarit 264

    Sonora 265

    Zacatecas 267

Resources 269

Bibliography 271

Acknowledgments

My deepest appreciation to all of the following people who so generously contributed their photos, expertise, time, and personal collections for me to photograph, without whom this book could not have been written.

Thank you to Jason Badgley, my dear friend who took the time to send me so many fine agates and jaspers from his personal collection to photograph; Jeff Anderson, Doris and Jim Banks, Chuck Bennett, Mark Berreth & Von Anderson-Berreth, Grant Curtis, Lowell Foster, Jeff Goebel, Barbara Grill, Richard Hauck, Darren Jones, Teyet Kepling, Pat McMahan, Jim Puckett, Gary Rider, Rimrock Gems, Greg Rosenberg, Lance Shope, Spanish Stirrup Rock Shop, Mike Streeter, and Tom Shearer.

A very special thanks to Kim Behnert for all her assistance with the compilation of this book, and to her husband Marcel as well, for being such good and helpful friends.

Thank you to Charlie, Maggie, Bo, and Ozzie for their editorial expertise with the maintenance of agategrrrl.com while I have been preoccupied.

Thank you to my good Aussie buddies Darren Jones and Keith Osborn for not only being such fun rockhounding friends, but for all their love and support in all my endeavors.

All my love to my daughter Sharon Gardner, and to the best son-in-law in the world, Jeff Gardner.

Thank you to my best friend and craziest rockhound buddy in the world, Barbara Grill, for always being there in every way for me and for sharing so many fun and exciting rockhounding adventures for over twenty years that have truly been some of the very best times of my life.

If I have forgotten anyone, I sincerely apologize and will catch you on the next go round!

Introduction to the Agates and Jaspers of North America

Polished cabochon with white plume agate on a black basinite backing.

Patti Polk Collection

It is no secret that North America has an incredible abundance of distinctive, unique, and excitingly beautiful agates and jaspers that are found throughout the United States and its neighbors, Canada and Mexico. There is an almost endless variety of types, patterns, and colors of jaspers and agates that occur in practically every state in the U.S., and in the territories, states, and provinces of Canada and Mexico. Personally, as a passionately dedicated lover of agates and jaspers, it is my intent to make an attempt to share as much of this abundance of riches with you so that you, too, can enjoy even a portion of the amazingly diverse, sometimes rare, and very beautiful bounty of Mother Nature's gifts that exist right here in our own backyards.

I am a dyed-in-the-wool rockhound, and I love nothing more than exploring and prospecting for agates and jaspers out in nature with the earth, sunshine, fresh air, darting lizards, and silence. I have spent many years in the field fervently hand-collecting a few thousand or so agates and jaspers to add to my own collection, and as long as my back holds up I definitely hope to be able to continue to have many more years enjoying

My best rockhound buddy Barbara Grill, fully equipped to rock with red wagon and umbrella hat.

A druzy quartz-coated chalcedony Desert Rose from Apache Creek, New Mexico. Patti Polk Collection

A small sampling of some of the agates to be found in the author's yard. Patti Polk Collection

the wonderfully crazy hobby of rock collecting. Don't get me wrong, I certainly don't claim to be an expert or a professional geologist – I'm just an avid rockhound who loves collecting agates and jaspers for their beauty and for the joy of the collecting experience, and I am constantly in the process of learning something new about the collecting, characteristics, and lapidary properties of agates and jaspers every day.

Most of my personal field-collecting experience takes place in Arizona, southern California, and New Mexico. As an agate collector, I'm very lucky in the fact that the west and southwest tend to be of the right type of geology that has a good number of locations conducive to the formation of so many fine agates and jaspers. In other words, volcanic environments that occurred during the right geologic time period to create the ideal environment that allows them to form here.

This book is by no means all-inclusive of all known collecting locations, or of every type of agate and jasper, nor is it a textbook on the geology of North America. It is simply a book written to share some examples that showcase the beauty and variety of the agates and jaspers that can generally be found on the North American continent. There are thousands of known locations in the United States alone, and many private locations that are not well known or publicized – and many unknown locations still waiting to be discovered by the serious prospector. Even within a specific location, there may be numerous deposits with variations of patterns

WARNING!
ROCK POX
Very Contagious to Both Sexes

SYMPTOMS — Continual complaint as to need for fresh air, sunshine, and relaxation. Patient has blank expression, sometimes inattentive to rest of family. Has no taste for work of any kind. Frequent checking of dealers' catalogs, and lapidary and mineral shops longer than usual. Secret phone calls to rock pals. Mumbles to self. Lies to rival collectors. Only one cure.

TREATMENT — Medication is useless. Disease is not fatal. Victim should go hunting as often as possible at beach, mountain, or desert hunting grounds. NOTE — If Dad and Mother both get it they just as well sell the home and buy a Camper.

Funny clipping from an old 1940's rockhound magazine. Still true today! Patti Polk Collection

Arizona rockhounding country. Darren Jones image, Patti Polk Collection

or color within just a couple hundred yards of each other. It truly is an amazing experience to dig just under the surface of the earth and pull out a mysterious, ancient agate and to know that you are the very first person who has ever held it in their hand or seen its unique beauty.

If I am able to share even a tiny bit of my enthusiasm and deep appreciation of these great natural treasures with you, then my job is done. If you are new to the world of agate and jasper collecting, be prepared to have your eyes opened to a palette of vibrant color, infinite pattern, and displays of some of the finest art found in all of nature. If you are a seasoned collector, I hope that you sit back and enjoy some of the old favorites, and just maybe, a few new surprises.

The author in her element. Kim Behnert image, Patti Polk Collection

Agate carving. Patti Polk Collection

History, Folklore and Use of Agates and Jaspers

Agates and jaspers have a long history of use worldwide by mankind. Historians have dated the use of cryptocrystalline materials as early as 2 million years ago where prehistoric man first learned that by chipping away at the edges of hard rocks that useful tools and weapons could be fashioned. In Lower Paleolithic times, 100,000 - 500,000 years ago, throughout Africa, Europe, and Asia, people were creating pebble tools, hand axes, hammerstones, flaked tools and blade tools. By the Upper Paleolithic period, tool making had evolved into finely crafted spearpoints and knives. Ancient agate artifacts have been discovered in Mongolia, Western Europe, and Asia dating back as far as 9,000 years. The Sumerians of Mesopotamia were the first people recognized for mastering the use of agate in the creation of ornamental beads, signet rings, cylinder seals, and ceremonial axeheads dating back to at least 3000 B.C. The early Egyptians were also using agates for various types of ornamentation that they collected from surrounding desert areas, as were the Mycenaeans from Crete during the Bronze Age. The Romans also used agate in their jewelry, and the Greeks pioneered the use of banded agates in the carving of multi-layered cameos and carnelian, bloodstone, or sard for beautifully intricate intaglios. The first man known to write a recorded history on the use of agates was Theophrastus (372-287 B. C.), a

Chert arrowhead from Alabama. Patti Polk Collection

Carved red jasper bead.
Patti Polk Collection

Moss agate Native American knife tool.
Bloody Basin, Arizona. Patti Polk Collection

Greek philosopher and naturalist, who gave agate its original name "achate" from the agates discovered on the shore of the river Achates in Sicily. Theophrastus wrote in his treatise "On Stones" that agate was a beautiful stone that commanded a high price in his day. Pliny the Elder (23-79 A. D.) also wrote a great deal about the lore of agates in his chronicle "Natural History," where he goes into great detail about the use of agates, such as how certain agates protect against

Polished Utah Septarian Nodule decorative heart.
Patti Polk Collection

the scorpion's sting, quench your thirst when held in the mouth, and that the Persians believed that the perfume of agate could turn away powerful or violent storms, amongst many other claims. Fine drinking cups made of agate were held in the highest regard and it was a hallmark of great prestige to possess one.

In the Bible, in the 28th and 39th chapters of Exodus, there is a marvelous account of the divine direction that was given to high priest Aaron (brother of Moses) to create a very special breastplate of precious stones to memorialize the twelve tribes of Israel using a number of agates and jaspers as important stones in the making of the garment.

Agate was used in various forms during the Dark Ages as talismans or for good luck pieces and fine agate jewelry was prized in France and England throughout the 17th and 18th centuries. In the mid-19th and early 20th centuries, colorful Scottish agate gained popularity and was commonly used in fashionable Victorian and Art Nouveau jewelry worldwide.

One of the most famous locations in the world known for the production of agate as ornaments and gemstones is in the area of Idar-Oberstein in Germany. Idar-Oberstein has a recorded history of working with agates since the late 13th century, although it is believed that production began much earlier, dating back to Roman times. Idar-Oberstein was one of the main centers that made use of agate on an industrial scale. Originally, locally found agates were used to make all types of objects for the European market, but it became a globalized business around the turn of the 20th century when large quantities of agate from Brazil were imported into the country as ship's ballast. Idar-Oberstein remains an active agate manufacturing center today, with modern mechanized methods of cutting and polishing replacing the

Polished agate geode trinket box.
Patti Polk Collection

manually operated and labor-intensive methods of bygone times.

In North America, agates and jaspers have been used by native people since their arrival on this continent. Native Americans have used agate and jasper to make tools, weapons, and many different types of ornamental or ceremonial objects. Naturally smooth round river agates have been routinely used as tools for burnishing hides for leather making and also to create a shiny finished surface on their clay pottery. Agate, jasper, rhyolite, and chert have been used extensively in the making of tools such as axeheads, projectile points, spearpoints, hammerstones, adzes, scrapers, drills, hoes, grinding stones, and even fish hooks. Decorative or ceremonial objects include fetishes, beads, sculptural stones, bowls, knives, arrowheads, and body ornaments.

Agates were also in limited use by the early North American white settlers in the original colonies in the United States, and in the province of Nova Scotia in Canada. Early sources of agates were known by the mid-1700s in the eastern U.S. in New York, New Jersey, Connecticut, and Rhode Island. The Aztecs of Mexico occasionally used small pieces of agate and jasper in their jewelry and ornaments. In the late 19th century in America, costume jewelry set with agate became popular due to the discovery of the Lake Superior agates in the Great Lakes region and from the Brazilian agate coming from the German supplies of Idar-Oberstein. As agate gained greater popularity in jewelry-making, amateur collectors began to search for the gemstones themselves and the hobby of agate and jasper collecting was born in North America. As the interest in collecting agates grew, people began publishing books and magazines about rock and mineral collecting, of which the collecting of agates and jaspers was a major component. One of the first periodicals in North America to be published was *Rocks and Minerals* magazine in 1927, followed by *Desert* magazine in 1937 - one of the very first publications to actually provide information

about collecting locations in the U.S. In 1947, *Lapidary Journal* came into existence and taught people not only how and where to collect gemstones, but also how to cut and polish the rocks that they found. Many other books and magazines have followed in their footsteps over the

Zuni carved jasper horned toad. Patti Polk Collection

ensuing years, and currently there is an abundance of written reference material available for anyone who has an interest in the lapidary arts or in the collecting of rocks such as agates and jaspers. Since World War II, collecting rocks has flourished as a popular hobby for rockhounds of all ages, and rock collecting clubs are in existence throughout the U.S., Canada, and Mexico.

Today, agates and jaspers are used primarily for the purpose of jewelry making in the form of polished cabochons and beads, as decorative items,

The author's much used Genie polishing unit. Patti Polk Collection

or as polished specimens for collectors. Agates and jaspers have long been a favorite of craftspeople for all types of art projects, including a fantastic set of six large agate windows hand made from local beach pebbles for a church in Yachats, OR, or as beautiful accent pieces often used in the making of stained glass windows or lampshades.

FOLKLORE

Throughout history, agates and jaspers have been believed to possess talismanic, metaphysical, and healing powers, including the ability to protect the wearer from danger, enhance memory and concentration, promote calmness, and act as a grounding stone for people who need increased stability in their lives. Historically, in the Middle East, Mediterranean, and Indo-European societies, banded or eye agates that were cut properly to expose their concentric circles were believed to ward off the "evil eye" if worn as a protective amulet. In modern times, agate is recognized as an appropriate gemstone for the 12th and 14th wedding anniversaries, and agate and jasper are both used as birthstones for the astrological signs of Virgo, Gemini, and Capricorn. For Virgos: carnelian, moss agate, and jasper; for Gemini: any type of agate; for Capricorn: any type of agate.

Picture jasper donut bead for jewelry making. Patti Polk Collection

Our 31st president, Herbert Hoover, collected agates as a child near his boyhood home in West Branch, Iowa, and, after graduating from Stanford University in 1895 with a geology degree, spent the next two decades as a mining engineer and is the only geologist to become an American president. Hoover's boyhood enthusiasm is aptly evidenced by this quote: "… on industrious search, you discovered gems of agate and fossil coral which could with infinite

Agate arrow point. 3", Utah. Patti Polk image, Doris Banks Collection

backaches be polished on the grindstone. Their fine points came out wonderfully when wet, and you had to lick them with your tongue before each exhibit." Still so true today, as any agate field collector knows.

There are also many agates and jaspers in the United States that are recognized as state rocks or gemstones, including: Arizona: petrified wood, Fire Agate; Florida: Agatized Coral; Kentucky: Kentucky Agate; Louisiana: Agate; Maryland: Patuxent River Stone; Michigan: Petoskey Stone (fossilized coral); Minnesota: Lake Superior Agate; Mississippi: petrified wood; Missouri: Mozarkite; Montana: Montana Agate; Nebraska: Nebraska Blue Agate, Prairie Agate; Ohio: flint; Oregon: Agate Thunderegg; South Dakota: Fairburn Agate; Tennessee: Tennessee Paint Rock; Texas: petrified palmwood; Washington: petrified wood; West Virginia: fossil coral. In Canada, agate is the official gemstone of Nova Scotia.

LAPIDARY USES

In today's world, agates and jaspers are highly desirable for many lapidary uses due to their beauty, versatility, durability, and ability to take a good polish. Agates and jaspers are routinely cut into strikingly beautiful cabochons for jewelry settings, such as rings, bracelets, pendants or earrings, and also made into beads for stringing in necklaces or other jewelry components.

Hand-wrought copper lamp with Arizona petrified wood lampshade. Greg Rosenberg image

Agate and copper woven wire
necklace made by the author.
Patti Polk Collection

Top quality agates and jaspers are also either face polished on a flat lap or dome polished on a polishing arbor to be added as prized specimens for collectors to display in their collections. Worldwide, there are private collectors who have only the most beautiful and finest agates and jaspers in their museum-quality collections worth well into the hundreds of thousands of dollars, as well as us regular old rockhounds who love their pretty rocks just as much as the most expensive collector piece even if there's not a big financial value attached to them.

Agates and jaspers are used in the production of many different decorative items such as carvings, sculptures, bookends, obelisks, pyramids, spheres, eggs, candleholders, and boxes. Slices are often used for wind chimes or in many other kinds of craft projects. Flintknapping is also a popular craft practiced by skilled artisans utilizing flint, chert, jasper, agate, and obsidian in the making of their beautiful, finely honed arrowheads and spearpoints as fascinating display specimens.

Information on the
Properties of Agates and Jaspers

Enhydro agate from Malibu Beach, California. The water-trapped air bubble is visible within the circle.

Patti Polk image, Jason Badgley Collection

On the continent of North America, there is a tremendous variety of collectible agates and jaspers available to the interested collector, whether personally hand dug in the field or acquired through rock shops, rock shows, rock clubs, or by online sources. Whether you are field collecting or purchasing your materials, you need to be aware of a number of different things, depending on what your particular use or interest is in relation to the stones you are getting. If you are a beginning collector and want to try your hand at field collecting, you will need to learn the basics of what the different types of agates and jaspers look like so you can begin to identify them, and how to determine where to find them. If you are a lapidary artist and want to use them for jewelry-making or other decorative applications, you will need to learn about their physical properties to be able to select and work with them properly. And if you are a collector who enjoys them for their beauty, particular type of pattern, or rarity, you naturally will want to understand their origins and locations so that you can be knowledgeable about your collection.

Basically, agates and jaspers are formed as fine-grained cryptocrystalline quartz composed of silicon dioxide (Si02). The most basic form of cryptocrystalline quartz is called chalcedony (pronounced kal-sid-nee). Pure chalcedony is nearly colorless and translucent, but can be colored, banded, and patterned when included with other minerals. When chalcedony has distinctive bands or patterns on a clear or translucent background it is known as agate. When chalcedony is so infiltrated with mineral impurities that it becomes opaque, or nearly so, it is then called jasper. Chert and flint also fall under the category of jasper. Sometimes all three types may be contained in one rock, such as a jasp-agate with some clear translucent areas of chalcedony, areas with agate banding, and opaque jasper or chert sections. Chalcedony, agate, and jasper are among the most favored materials for lapidary use due to their exquisite colors and patterns, excellent hardness, durability, and ability to take a high polish. On the Mohs scale, agates and jaspers fall generally between 6.5-7 on the hardness scale. Agates are usually around 7, and jaspers are often somewhat softer and more porous than agates due to their higher earthy mineral content. Some of the most common mineral inclusions in agate and jasper are manganese, iron oxide, chromium, celadonite, nickel, copper, hematite, and sometimes uranium (which gives the beautiful petrified rainbow woods of Arizona and Utah their brilliant yellow colors).

Plumes in agate, West Texas. Patti Polk Collection

Agates and jaspers form in fairly specific environments, primarily volcanic andesites, rhyolites, and tholeiitic basalts, or in sedimentary limestones and claystones. There is still much scientific debate about the exact nature of how certain agates and jaspers form, but there are several generally accepted theories about their origins. In simple terms, most agates form within gas pockets, cracks, or fissures in cooled lavas that are infiltrated and filled over time with percolating waters carrying silica gel and other minerals. Agates usually form as amygdaloidal (almond shaped) nodules, or as veins in fissures. Chalcedony, the building block of agate, can also act as a replacement of another

Crystal druzy coating on plume agate, Brenda, Arizona. Patti Polk Collection

Agate pseudomorph, Black Canyon, Arizona. Patti Polk Collection

material, such as organic matter, or of other minerals, which results in specimens of petrified wood and dinosaur bone, or such as agate after barite or aragonite pseudomorphs. Thundereggs are a type of agate surrounded by a relatively thick rhyolitic rind or casing, and frequently exhibit a solid star-shaped pattern within the center of the rock. Geodes are generally round in form and may have a thin to thick layer of agate along the inside wall that contains a hollow center often lined with sparkling quartz crystals.

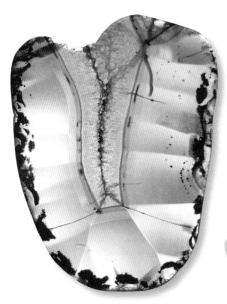

Backlit agate slab exhibiting a turtleback effect, Montana. Patti Polk Collection

Chalcedony replacement limb cast with small branch knob, Wyoming. Patti Polk Collection

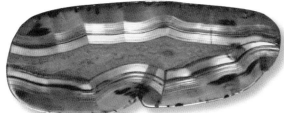

Iris effect in Montana agate.
Gary Rider Collection

AGATE AND JASPER TERMINOLOGY

Agates and jaspers can go by many different names due to their numerous variations of pattern and color, localities, and geographic locations. Some agates and jaspers have very well-defined names recognized by their known locations, such as Owyhee Jasper from Oregon or Laguna Agate from Mexico; or others recognized by their pattern and color, such as Crazy Lace Agate or Picture Jasper. The names of agates and jaspers can sometimes be confusing though and seemingly arbitrary, depending on whom is doing the naming and if the material is from an old, new, or unknown location. Usually most agates and jaspers do come from known locations and the first way to begin to identify them is by looking at their patterns and colors, and that is a good starting point in determining what location they might have come from if you don't already know.

Commonly Found Patterns Occurring in Agate and Jasper

PATTERN	DESCRIPTION
Aggregate Stalks	Fingerlike structures in a row emanating from one direction on one plane.
Banded	Smooth, concentric, unbroken rings.
Brecciated or Ruin	Broken fragments re-cemented into a random pattern.
Cloud	Cloud-like wispy patterns, often found in chalcedony.
Dendritic	Two dimensional tree or branchlike inclusions.
Dot	Small solid round dots, like a polka dot.
Egg or Ovoid	Undulating or overlapping oval patterns resembling eggs.
Eye or Orbicular	Small concentric rings or circles, like an eye. Spherulites.
Flame	Upright, fiery structures that look like flames.
Floater	Small floating banded section in the center of a nodule surrounded by euhedral quartz.
Flower or Bouquet	Singular flowers or groups of puffy clusters resembling flower bouquets.
Fortification	Concentric rings with complex angular or curving patterns.
Lace	Delicate, lacy patterns throughout.
Lattice	Angular, bladed sections in a zigzag or lattice-like pattern.
Moss	Strings, seaweed, or mossy looking inclusions.
Mottled	Irregularly marked with splotches of color.
Plume	Single, three-dimensional feather-like inclusions.
Pom Pom	A small fluffy looking ball composed of radiating sagenite needles.
Sagenite	Sprays of needles, hairlike, or fan-like inclusions.
Scenic or Picture	Patterns or lines that resemble landscape formations.
Snowflake	Small floating groups of dots or flakes like snow.
Spiderweb	Crisscross or woven patterns like a spider web.
Tube	Elongated tube-like structures, usually with internal concentric rings.
Waterline or Onyx	Straight, parallel lines of banding.

Beautiful lavender fortification banded agate geode with quartz crystal center and parallax shadowing in the bands, Laguna, Mexico. Patti Polk Collection

Exterior view of a geode, Wiley Wells, California. Patti Polk Collection

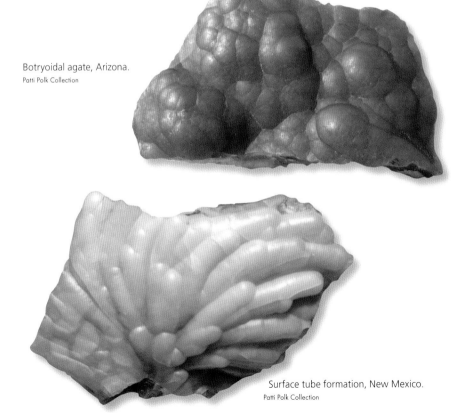

Botryoidal agate, Arizona.
Patti Polk Collection

Surface tube formation, New Mexico.
Patti Polk Collection

Information on the Properties of Agates & Jaspers | **21**

Small golden sagenite sprays in agate. Patti Polk Collection

Physical Forms of Agate and Jasper

Shown here are the most common forms, structures, or environments of Agate and Jasper.

FORM	DESCRIPTION
Botryoidal	Chalcedony that is shaped like bubbles or clusters of grapes. Often a surface coating.
Geode	Round rock with an open center cavity, often quartz crystal-lined.
Jasp-Agate	A mixture of both translucent agate and opaque jasper within one stone.
Limb Cast	Chalcedony wood replacement created by a mold left from an original decomposed limb.
Massive	An amorphous structure, thick and dense; often in large solid chunks or seams.
Nodule	Rock with an agatized center, almond, oval or football shaped; Amygdaloidal.
Polyhedral	A sharply geometric or angularly shaped nodule.
Pseudomorph	Silica or another mineral replacing and taking the form of a previous mineral.
Sedimentary	Nodules or thundereggs formed in marine layer deposits, such as limestone or claystone.
Thunderegg	Round rock with a solid agatized internal center cavity surrounded by matrix, often in a star shaped pattern.
Vein	Rock formed within a crack or fissure, flat or rectangular shaped.
Volcanic	Nodules or veins formed in volcanic lavas such as rhyolite, basalt, or andesite.

Rough cut slab showing dendrites, Nevada.
Patti Polk Collection

Rough chunk of agate with large spherulitic snowflakes, Apache Creek, New Mexico. Patti Polk Collection

Common and Unusual Characteristics

A variety of characteristics found in agates and jaspers, some common and some rare, such as Iris agate.

CHARACTERISTIC	DESCRIPTION
Chromatography	A dramatic shift in color within a region of banding in an agate.
Druze or Druzy	A coating of fine quartz crystals on the surface of an agate or within a geode.
Enhydro	Solid agate with an internal water-filled cavity, often with a visible air bubble. Fairly rare.
Fire	Displays shimmering iridescence within surface layers, such as Fire Agate.
Fluorescent	Exhibits bright neon colors under ultraviolet light in darkness.
Iris	Agate when cut very thin and backlit displays the color spectrum within its bands. Rare.
Opalescence	Displays fiery flashes of color within surface layers, such as is seen in precious Opal.
Parallax	Moving, shadowy effect exposed within tight agate banding when rotated.
Petrification	The replacement of organic matter by chalcedony, but retaining its original structure.
Turtleback	Turtleshell pattern displayed in clear agate when backlit.

There are many excellent books written in great depth specifically on the subjects of agate and jasper identification, and on the scientific theories that discuss the genesis, geologic formation, and chemical characteristics of agates and jaspers in the U.S. and worldwide. These may be found online, in bookstores, and some are listed in the resources section of this book.

Typical agate collecting country near Bouse, Arizona. Patti Polk Collection

Collecting the Agates and Jaspers of North America

Agates and jaspers are probably the most commonly collected variety of rocks in the history of mankind due to their incredible variety, beautiful patterns and colors, durability for lapidary applications, and their overall accessibility. Agates and jaspers are found all over the world, in every country and on every continent. Some are exceedingly rare and quite expensive, while others are readily available for collecting or purchasing and very affordable for anyone who would like to possess a pretty rock for display or jewelry-making.

Although mineralogical societies were in existence as early as 1885 in the U.S., the hobby of rock collecting as we know it today in the United States really began in the 1930s during the Great Depression as unemployed people searching for gold in California found other interesting rocks, such as agate, jasper, and petrified wood, and brought them home as collectible items. Word spread amongst like-minded collectors and jewelry makers and groups began to form to share information about the different types of collectible materials and favorite collecting locations.

In the early 1930s, a number of rock clubs were formed, primarily in California along the Pacific Coast and into Oregon, and as the interest in collecting grew, so did the question of what to do with all the rocks that people were collecting. People began to share information with each other within the clubs about gem-cutting techniques and the art of amateur lapidary was born. Clubs also began to organize field trips to local areas where members would be guaranteed to find some good materials for their purposes. Since those early days, hundreds of clubs have sprung up over the years and even today, you can still find clubs in almost every state in the U.S. and Canada.

If you are new to the world of agate and jasper collecting, joining a rock club is an excellent place to start. Clubs offer the opportunity to go out on field trips with experienced collectors so you can learn about how to collect what you want in the field, what to look for, and how to identify what you're finding. You can learn about local rocks and other materials at the monthly club meetings where there are educational programs and speakers offering their knowledge and expertise on the subject. If you aren't interested in joining a group and want to try exploring on your own, there are many fine trail guides available for just about every state in the U.S. and Canada. I personally don't endorse making any attempt to collect in Mexico on your own, as most areas in that country are under claim or on private ranches and your safety may be in question if you trespass. So, if you want to collect Mexican agates and jaspers, you will need to buy them from the mine owners, get permission from the ranch owners to collect on their property, or buy them from rock dealers at shows, rock shops, or online.

My good buddy Jason Badgley out field collecting in the Malibu Hills, California. Rick Montgomery image, Jason Badgley Collection

Small agate nodules in
basalt matrix. Patti Polk Collection

Agate vein in rhyolite matrix, South Cady Mountains, California. Patti Polk Collection

If you want to get out on your own in the field to collect agates and jaspers, you will need to start with either a known location or an educated guess about an unknown location. You can get information on known locations from other rock collectors, clubs, or from rock collecting trail guides such as *Gem Trails of Utah*, the *Rockhound's Guide to New Mexico*, and so on. Any of these books are easily found online or at most major bookstores. If you want to prospect for a new location yourself, you will have to have some kind of an understanding of the geology of the area that will produce the agate or jasper that you are looking for. Agates and jaspers usually form in volcanic andesites, rhyolites, and basalts, or in

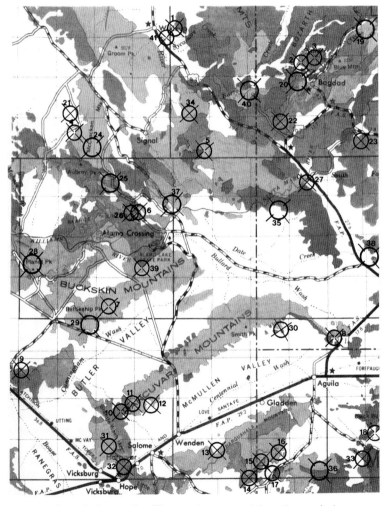

A section of a geologic map. The different colors represent the various geologic ages.
Patti Polk Collection

certain sedimentary deposits such as limestone or claystone. Depending on what area of the country you live in, you will also want to be aware of the geologic time period that they were likely to have formed in. For example, here in Arizona, petrified wood formed in the Late Triassic period and is found in the sedimentary layers of the Chinle Formation. You will need to do your own research to determine where the most likely location is in your area to find whatever it is that you are looking for. You can order geologic maps for every state in the U.S. from the U.S. Geological Survey, and for Canada from the Geological Survey of Canada. Both websites are listed in the resources section of this book.

You can also start from a known location and explore adjacent areas. Often, agate and jasper deposits will lie along the same elevation, so you can follow a topographic map line along a particular elevation for many miles, and with any luck, you may run across a new deposit. There's never any guarantee though that you will find something just because the area looks right – I personally have hiked many, many long miles over hill and dale and haven't always been rewarded for my hard work. But, occasionally you do find a new, unexplored agate field and it is beyond description how incredibly wonderful it is to look down on the ground and see it littered with untouched, beautiful agates just laying on the surface waiting for you to be the very first one to pick them up.

Whether you choose to go collecting out on your own or with other people, safety has to always be a paramount consideration, especially if you are going to a remote region. A good 4-wheel-drive vehicle is always the most desirable if you are going on rough, unknown, or unmaintained roads, and you should always wear a good pair of gloves and safety glasses when wielding a hammer, pick or shovel. I generally don't recommend going out alone, but if you do decide to, always let someone know where you are and when you expect to be home. Always bring plenty of water and gas, proper clothing,

Colorful petrified wood in place on a privately owned ranch (now closed) near Holbrook, Arizona.
Patti Polk Collection

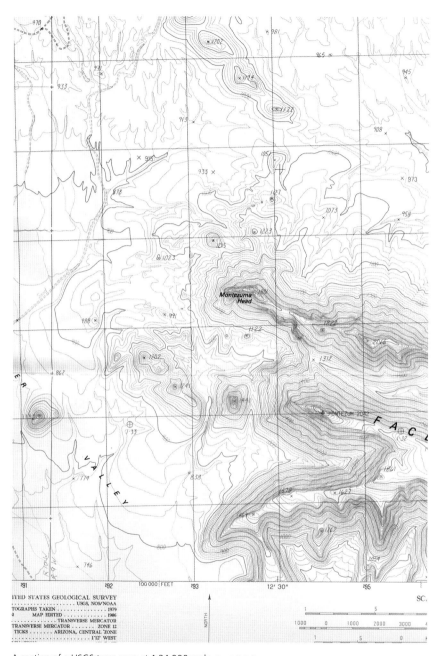

A section of a USGS topo map at 1:24 000 scale. Patti Polk Collection

food, a cell phone or walkie-talkie, and don't ever take any unnecessary risks, like leaning over an unstable overhang to get that one last shining agate calling your name, just out of reach.

It is also important to remember to be a courteous and conscientious field collector. If you dig holes, fill them. If you have trash, carry it out. If you open a gate, close it behind you. Don't be a hog and take everything in sight – leave something for the next person to find. Collecting responsibly ensures that our hobby will be able to continue to survive for years to come. Unfortunately, we have already lost a good number of great collecting locations directly as a result of the reasons I just mentioned, so let's make a concentrated effort to prevent that from happening in the future.

If you want to learn about the geology of your region, a good place to visit is any local natural history museums that would have examples of what can be found in your state. For beginning collectors, there are also a great series of books called *Roadside Geology* and *Geology Underfoot* that cover many of the states in the U.S., and a good one for Canada is *Canada Rocks: The Geologic Journey*. All of these books are excellent places to start learning about the geology of your area so you can begin to experience your own rockhounding adventures.

AGATE AND JASPER OF THE U.S., CANADA, & MEXICO

In the sections on the United States, Canada, and Mexico, I give a brief overview of the geology of each state, province, or territory. Some U.S. states have a great many collecting locations for agate and jasper, and some may have very little or none at all, depending on the geology of the region. In the eastern U.S., there is little in the way of agate as that area is primarily a metamorphic, granitic region that is not appropriate to the formation of agate. There are some small exceptions to the rule, though, and sometimes agates and jaspers can be found in locations where they didn't originate, but were brought there through other means such as glaciation or deposition by oceans, rivers, and streams.

In this section, in an effort to show as many varieties of agate and jasper types as possible, I step outside the bounds of the strict definition of an agate or jasper and include many kinds of chalcedony-included materials that can fall into the category of a chalcedony, agate, jasper, flint, chert, rhyolite, fossil, or opalite due to their cryptocrystalline structure and silica content. And, although obsidian is silica-rich, by definition it is really a volcanic glass that falls into a category of its own, so I will not be not including it in this book at this time.

It is not realistic to attempt to include photos of every single type of agate and jasper in North America that is known to exist, or has existed, in this book, but I will do my best to show as many examples as is feasible to give you an idea of what can reasonably be found in a state or region. I will show photos of materials from well known collecting locations as well as some unusual, extinct, or private collecting areas. For historical value, I will show some materials that can no longer be found due to a variety of reasons, such as areas being mined out, closed and designated as new wilderness areas, or covered over and developed as private properties. Collecting location access, laws, and designation can change in the blink of an eye, so it is your responsibility to know the status of the land where you would like to do your collecting. You need to know if it is private property, under claim, or BLM, state or forest land. You don't want to be caught trespassing or collecting where you're not supposed to be. A number of states now have stiff fines if they catch you collecting in a prohibited area, and some can even confiscate your property if they really want to give you a hard time. Luckily, there are also many privately owned fee-based collecting sites in the U.S. where you pay a fixed amount for whatever you collect during the course of the day.

Large agatized dinosaur femur bone collected in the 1950s, 18" tall, 80 pounds. It is not possible to collect specimens like this today due to restrictive new laws and lack of land access. Patti Polk image, Doris Banks Collection

In some instances, I will show the cut front face of an agate or jasper and also a second photo showing the rough exterior of the same piece so you can see what they look like naturally in the field. Often, out in the field, the exteriors of agates and jaspers can be deceptive and look completely different from what is on the inside due to oxidation, weathering, or just by the nature of the formation of their rind or skin. Most of the time you wouldn't have any idea that there would

Just one of the many different state-by-state collecting location guides available to collectors both online and at major bookstores. Patti Polk Collection

be anything of interest or beauty inside them unless you see a chipped edge or broken surface that exposes their lovely interior. Also, exterior characteristics can vary considerably depending on where you're collecting and what kind of terrain or deposit you are collecting in.

The photos in this section include shots of natural rough material, faced material (rough material that has been cut to expose the interior of the rock), polished and unpolished slabs, polished specimen pieces, and polished cabochons. On some unpolished slabs or rough, I have lightly oiled the surface to bring out a little more of the color in the same way that the color is brightened when the material is polished. Some specimens are simple and humble examples of what can be found in an area, while others may be top-notch collector pieces that are truly exceptional and quite difficult to come by, unless you have large dollars to spend.

When known, I have included the measurements of the pieces and are as follows: widest point across the face by the highest point across the face by the depth or length of the piece. Locations are arranged by country, state, locality if known, and by county. In some states, there are numerous counties that contain the same types of material, so I mention only the most important ones. If you are looking for directions to specific collecting locations, you can find them in your state's field collecting guidebooks, through local rock clubs, or through online sources.

Values are given per specimen piece, unless listed as per pound. Agate and jasper values can vary greatly depending on rarity, quality, size, condition, region, market demand, seller pricing practices, and whether it is rough, cut, or polished. Prices included here are general, averaged retail prices that a buyer would expect to pay for mid-grade material from a rock dealer online, or at a gem and mineral show at current market rates.

I hope you enjoy as much as I do the beauty, wonder, and mystery of some of Mother Earth's finest treasures, found right here under our feet.

Alabama

For more information about geology, mineralogy, paleontology and lapidary arts, visit the Alabama Mineral and Lapidary Society at www.lapidaryclub.com.

The northern half of Alabama is comprised of sedimentary beds containing coal, iron, and limestone caverns. The southern half is mostly sedimentary rock with a base of sand and gravel. In the Tuscaloosa Formation, about 500 feet above sea level, there are deposits of chert that have been used by native peoples for tool-making since earliest times. Metamorphic rock formations in the east central area of the state also offer opportunities for gem collecting. For agate and jasper collectors, Alabama is best known for its Paint Rock agate, situated in Jackson County. Carnelian, chert, and agate pebbles may be found in gravel pits in Franklin and Blount counties, and quartz geodes occur west of Athens in Limestone County. Tallahatta Chert, popular for flintknapping, can be found in Clarke and Washington counties in fields and river channels. Fossil sponge has been reported near Fort Payne in DeKalb County, and petrified wood can be found in Tuscaloosa County, along with sagenite agate near Brookwood.

▲ Alabama jasp-agate slab, unknown location, **$5**. Patti Polk image, Pat McMahan Collection

▲ Native American chert tool, 2.5" x 2" x .25", **$10**. Patti Polk Collection

▲ Paint Rock agate, Greasy Cove, Etowah County, **$45**. Jeff Anderson Collection

Alaska

For more information about mineral collecting and lapidary in Alaska, visit www.chugachgms.org.

Alaska, the largest state in the U.S., has quite a complex topography. The Pacific coast is bordered by mountains that are formed of sedimentary rocks with igneous intrusions. These mountain ranges include active volcanoes and Mt. McKinley, the highest peak in North America. In the southeast are rugged mountains, fjords, and islands. The central area has placer gold streams and open tundras at sea level. The Aleutians are a volcanically active chain of islands in the southwest. The northeast has vast, great plains similar to the plains of the Midwest in the lower 48 states. Gold and ore minerals are abundant in many areas of the state, as well as jade in the upper northwest region. Agate and jasper collecting opportunities occur primarily on the

▲ Multi-layer agate with quartz crystals, Wrangell Island, 5" x 2.5" x 4", **$15**. Patti Polk Collection

beaches from Gambier Bay to Wilson Cove and Point Gardner, Admiralty Island; near Anchorage, along the Matahuska and Kenai Rivers and the beaches of Kenai Peninsula on Cook Inlet; Popof Island, near Sand Point; Port Heiden beaches, Alaska

▲ Banded beach agate, Kenai Peninsula, 1" x .75" x 1", **$1**. Patti Polk Collection

Peninsula; and Wrangell, at Agony Beach. Agate, carnelian, jasper, and chalcedony pebbles can be found on many beaches in the Aleutian Islands including Adak, Attu, Shumagin, Tanaga, and Unalaska Islands. Petrified wood can be found in the Anchor River near Anchorage, and Bristol Bay, Wrangell, and Unga Island locations. Hollow blue agates have reportedly been found in the Talkeetna area in the Matanuska-Susitna Borough.

▶ Banded beach agate, Anchor Point, Kenai Peninsula, 1.5" x 1" x 1.25", **$3**. Patti Polk Collection

Arizona

For more information about agates and jaspers in Arizona, visit author Patti Polk's site at agategrrrl.com.

Arizona is one of the most heavily mineralized states in the U.S. Often called the "Copper State," its high-forested plateaus, arid desert plains, and southern riparian areas offer a wide and diverse topography. The Colorado Plateau extends over the northern third of the state, and its ancient sandstone formations offer the rockhound many collecting opportunities for petrified wood, agates, jaspers, and various fossils in the eroded sediments and river gravels. The central and southern portion of the state below the Mogollon Rim is a semi-arid desert region rich in low volcanic mountains from which many collectible chalcedony minerals erode. Agate and jasper occur in practically every county in Arizona. Some popular agate and jasper collecting locations include Brenda, Yuma County; Alpine, Apache County; Clifton, Greenlee County; Burro Creek, Yavapai County; and Tonopah, Maricopa County. Many types of agates, jaspers, fossils, and petrified woods can be collected all the way from Yuma to Bullhead City in the ancient river gravel bars along the Colorado River. Fire agate can be collected at the BLM managed Black Hills Rockhound Park near Safford in Greenlee County, or at a fee-based mine near Oatman in Mohave County.

▲ Polished fire agate cabochon from agate collected at Black Hills Rockhound Park, Graham County, .75" x .5" x .25", **$30**. Patti Polk Collection

▲ Petrified wood with botryoidal surface, Navajo County, 4" x 2" x 1", **$4 per pound**. Patti Polk Collection

◀ Rough Arizona Picture Wood, Navajo County, 4" x 2" x 1", **$8 per pound**.
Patti Polk Collection

▲ Petrified wood with quartz crystal coatings, Holbrook, Navajo County, 4" x 2.5" x 1", **$2 per pound**. Patti Polk Collection

◀ Rainbow wood rough round, Navajo County, 5" x 5" x 6", **$4 per pound**. Patti Polk Collection

▶ Green petrified wood, Navajo Indian Reservation, 1.5" x 1.25" x 1", **$25**. Patti Polk Collection

▲ Bacon agate, Graham County, 3.5" x 1.5" x 2", **$2 per pound**. Patti Polk Collection

▶ Dome polished fortification agate, Maricopa County, 2.5" x 2" x 2", **$20.**
Patti Polk Collection

◀ Dome face polished banded agate with druzy center. Private property now closed to collecting, Yavapai County, **$25**.
Patti Polk Collection

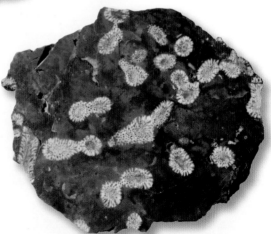

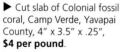

▶ Cut slab of Colonial fossil coral, Camp Verde, Yavapai County, 4" x 3.5" x .25", **$4 per pound**.
Patti Polk Collection

◄ Exterior of Colonial
fossil coral, 5" x 3.5" x 4".
Patti Polk Collection

► Agatized fossil
brachiopod, Springerville,
Apache County, 2" x 1.5" x 1.5",
$1 per pound. Patti Polk Collection

◄ Fossil sponge in chert,
Coconino County, 5" x 4" x 2",
$1 per pound. Patti Polk Collection

▶ Exterior of rough moss agate.
Patti Polk Collection

▲ Face cut rough moss agate, Yavapai County, 3″ x 3″ x 2″, **$8 per pound**. Patti Polk Collection

▲ Dome polished fortification and moss agate, Brenda, La Paz County; **$8 per pound**.
Patti Polk Collection

▲ Agate in float, Brenda, Arizona. Patti Polk Collection

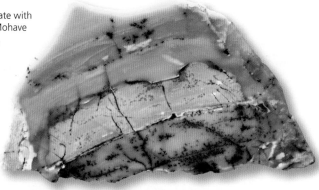

▶ Slab of dendritic agate with opalite, Burro Creek, Mohave County, 5.5" x 3" x 2", **$5 per pound**.
Patti Polk Collection

◀ Mushroom rhyolite slab, Aguila, Maricopa County, 6" x 4" x .25", **$5 per pound**. Patti Polk Collection

▲ Brecciated agate, Burro Creek, Mohave County, 5.5" x 3" x 3", **$5 per pound**. Patti Polk Collection

Arizona

◀ Rough purple agate interior with altered bentonite clay exterior, Burro Creek, Mohave County, 2" x 1" x 3", **$15 per pound**.
Patti Polk Collection

▶ Fossil Crinoid stems in jasper, Pine, Gila County, 4" x 3" x 2", **$2 per pound**. Patti Polk Collection

◀ Water-worn jasper pebble with Crinoid stem cast, Holbrook, Navajo County, 2" x 1.5" x 1", **$1**.
Patti Polk Collection

Arizona

▶ Rough flower agate. This site is now closed. Saint Johns, Apache County; **$12 per pound**. Patti Polk Collection

◀ Gem Silica with chrysocolla and malachite inclusions from the Morenci mine, Greenlee County; **$40**. Jeff Anderson Collection

▶ Large, colorful moss/plume agate rough, Bloody Basin, Yavapai County; **$12 per pound**. Patti Polk Collection

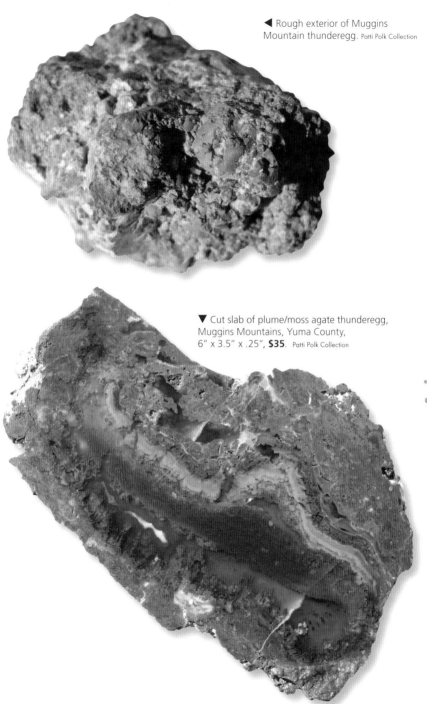

◄ Rough exterior of Muggins
Mountain thunderegg. Patti Polk Collection

▼ Cut slab of plume/moss agate thunderegg,
Muggins Mountains, Yuma County,
6" x 3.5" x .25", **$35**. Patti Polk Collection

Arizona

▶ Agate from Colorado River gravels, Bullhead City, Mohave County, 2.5" x 2" x 2.5", **$1 per pound**. Patti Polk Collection

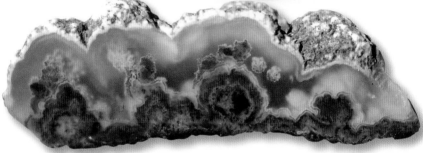

▲ Santa Maria River agate. Location now closed. Mohave County, 2" x .75" x 2", **$20 per pound**. Patti Polk Collection

▲ Moss/plume jasp-agate, Santa Cruz County, 3" x 2" x 1.5", **$20**. Patti Polk Collection

◀ Agate nodule, Peloncillo Mountains, Cochise County, 2″ x 2″ x 1.5″, **$2 per pound**. Patti Polk Collection

▶ Botryoidal chalcedony on rhyolite from the fire agate deposit near Oatman, Mohave County, 3″ x 2″ x 3″, **$10**.
Patti Polk Collection

◀ Sagenite agate with center fortification and druzy pocket, Sheep's Bridge, Yavapai County, 2.5″ x 2″ x 2″, **$20**.
Patti Polk Collection

▶ Face polished fortification agate nodule with sagenite, Yavapai County, 1.25″ x 1.25″ x 2″, **$20**.
Patti Polk Collection

◀ Orbicular rhyolite, Maricopa County, 3″ x 2″ x 2″, **$4 per pound**. Patti Polk Collection

▶ Antique Pink agate from Round Mountain, Greenlee County; **$45**.
Jeff Anderson Collection

Arizona

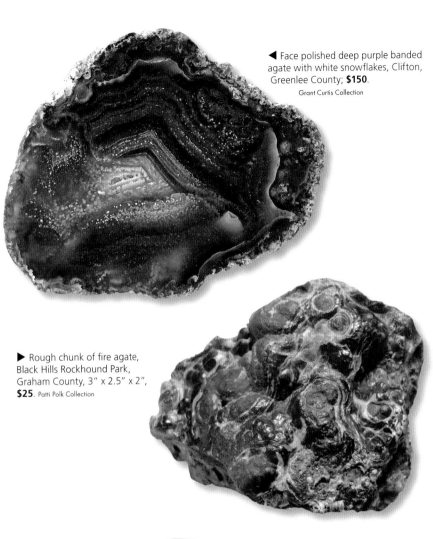

◀ Face polished deep purple banded agate with white snowflakes, Clifton, Greenlee County; **$150**.
Grant Curtis Collection

▶ Rough chunk of fire agate, Black Hills Rockhound Park, Graham County, 3" x 2.5" x 2", **$25**. Patti Polk Collection

◀ Rough banded hematite and jasper, Mingus Mountain, Yavapai County, 3" x 1" x 2", **$4 per pound**.
Patti Polk Collection

Arizona

▶ Fortification agate slab with parallax, tube, and moss inclusions, Tonopah, Maricopa County, 5" x 2.5" x .25", **$25**.
Patti Polk Collection

▶ Orbicular rhyolite from Colorado River gravels, Ehrenberg, La Paz County, 3.5" x 2.5" x .25", **$18**.
Patti Polk image, Jason Badgley Collection

▲ Rough oolitic agate with large orbs. Private property now closed to collecting, Yavapai County, 9" x 3" x 3", **$25**. Patti Polk Collection

Arkansas

For more information about rockhounding
and mineral collecting in Arkansas,
visit www.rockhoundingar.com.

Rugged mountain ranges including the Boston, Ozark, and
Ouachita, are the most important features of northwestern
Arkansas and are heavily mineralized. The Arkansas plateaus are
composed primarily of hard sedimentary rock while the counties
of Garland, Montgomery, Madison, Pike, Polk, and Hot Springs are
underlaid by areas of crystalline rock that created the state's famous
quartz crystal and diamond producing localities. The southern and
eastern corners are broad plains with sandy river deltas. Very good
lacy, banded agate known as Crowley Ridge agate comes from the
ancient floodplains of the Mississippi River near Forrest City in St.
Francis County. Also, in Craighead County, banded agates can be
found in the gravel beds, and banded chert occurs in Carroll County.

◄ Native American flint
tool, 3" x 1" x .5", **$5**.
Patti Polk Collection

▲ Native American chert tool, 3.25" x 1" x 1", **$5**. Patti Polk Collection

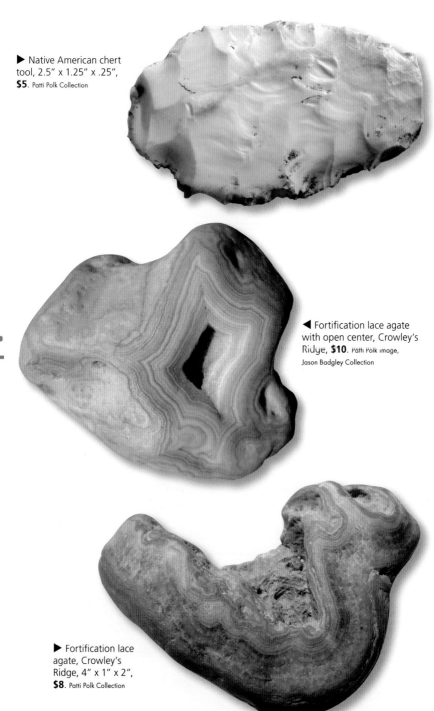

▶ Native American chert tool, 2.5″ x 1.25″ x .25″, **$5**. Patti Polk Collection

◀ Fortification lace agate with open center, Crowley's Ridge, **$10**. Patti Polk image, Jason Badgley Collection

▶ Fortification lace agate, Crowley's Ridge, 4″ x 1″ x 2″, **$8**. Patti Polk Collection

Arkansas

California

The California Federation of Mineralogical Societies includes more than 110 clubs and societies. For more information, visit www.cfmsinc.org.

California may be best known for its famous gold mines, but it holds many other agate and jasper treasures throughout the state as well. From the lowest point in Death Valley to the highest point of Mt. Whitney, it has everything from hot, barren deserts to lush, sweeping forests. In the north are glacier-cut valleys linked to Oregon's Cascade Mountains, and at its heart is a great central valley ringed with high mountains. To the west along the ocean lie the broken coastal ranges and to the east, the imposing Sierra Nevada mountain range looms along the border of neighboring Nevada. In the southeast region of the state lie the arid lands of the Great Basin, including the Mojave and Colorado deserts rich with agate deposits eroding from the ancient volcanic ranges and valleys. Many well-known agate collecting locations occur in Imperial, Inyo, Kern, Los Angeles, Riverside, San Bernardino, San Luis Obispo, and Santa Clara counties. Beach agates and fossils may be found at many of the beaches all along the coast from north to south, but many of California's collecting laws have recently changed, so be sure to check with the appropriate agencies and be aware of any legal restrictions in any area you are considering collecting in.

▲ Polished banded agate, Acton,
Los Angeles County, 6" x 3" x 1.25", **$30**.
Patti Polk image, Jason Badgley Collection

▶ Paul Bunyon tube agate slab,
Barstow, San Bernardino County,
4.5" x 2.5" x .25", **$20**.
Patti Polk image,
Jason Badgley Collection

California

▲ Dendritic agate slab, Valley Springs, Calaveras County, 5.25" x 2" x .25", **$10**.
Patti Polk image, Jason Badgley Collection

◀ Brecciated jasp-agate nodule, Van Duzen River, Humboldt County, 4" x 2" x 1.5", **$15**. Patti Polk Collection

▲ Lavender banded agate slab with parallax, North Cady Mountains, San Bernardino County, 3" x 1.5" x .25", **$40**. Patti Polk Collection

◀ Polished plume agate, Afton Canyon, San Bernardino County, 3" x 3" x 2", **$45**. Patti Polk image, Jason Badgley Collection

◀ Cut geode with druzy quartz center from the Hauser beds, Wiley's Well, Riverside County, 2.5" x 2.5" x 1.5", **$15.**
Patti Polk Collection

▶ Agate thunderegg, Black Beds deposit, Wiley's Well, Riverside County, 3" x 3" x 1.5", **$18**. Patti Polk image, Jason Badgley Collection

◀ Exterior of Cinnamon Bed geode. Patti Polk image, Jason Badgley Collection

▲ Agate geode with banding and quartz crystal pocket, Cinnamon Beds deposit, Wiley's Well, Riverside County, 3" x 3" x 2", **$15**. Patti Polk image, Jason Badgley Collection

▶ Polished fire agate cabochon, Coon Hollow, Riverside County, 1" x .5" x .25", **$40**.
Patti Polk Collection

◀ Rough scenic jasper, Wiley's Well, Riverside County, 2.5" x 2" x 3", **$15**.
Patti Polk image,
Jason Badgley Collection

California

▲ Unusual oolitic jasper slab, Essex, San Bernardino County, 5" x 1.5" x .25", **$20**. Patti Polk Collection

◄ Polished pigeon blood agate. Closed location. Fort Irwin, San Bernardino County, 3" x 3" x 2", **$20**.
Patti Polk image, Jason Badgley Collection

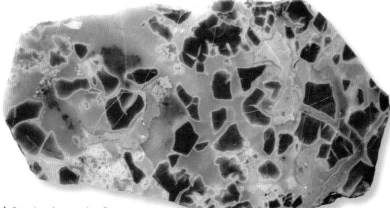

▲ Brecciated agate, Jacalitos Creek, Fresno County, 5" x 2.75" x 2", **$20**. Patti Polk image, Jason Badgley Collection

►Jasp-agate slab, Anderson Lake, Santa Clara County, 7" x 6.5" x .25", **$20**.
Patti Polk image, Jason Badgley Collection

▶ Rough exterior of Berkeley agate nodule, shown below.

Patti Polk image, Jason Badgley Collection

▼ Polished banded agate nodule, Berkeley, Alameda County, 4.25" x 2.25" x 2", **$20**.

Patti Polk image, Jason Badgley Collection

California

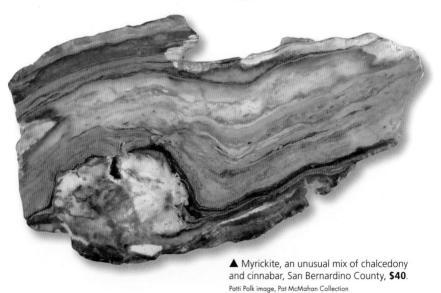

▲ Myrickite, an unusual mix of chalcedony and cinnabar, San Bernardino County, **$40**.

Patti Polk image, Pat McMahan Collection

◀ Horse Canyon moss agate slab, Tehachapi, Kern County, 3" x 2" x .25", **$18**. Patti Polk Collection

▶ Large multicolor Horse Canyon moss agate, Tehachapi, Kern County, 4.5" x 3.5" x 2.5", **$35**. Patti Polk Collection

◀ Exterior of large Horse Canyon agate. Patti Polk Collection

California

▶ Small rough piece of Needles blue agate, Needles, San Bernardino County, 1" x 1" x 1.5", **$25**. Patti Polk Collection

▲ Polished plume agate specimen from the Owlshead Mountains, San Bernardino County, **$50**. Patti Polk image, Pat McMahan Collection

◀ Exterior of Cambria thunderegg.
Patti Polk image, Jason Badgley Collection

▼ Banded agate suspended in quartz
thunderegg, Cambria, San Luis Obispo County,
4.5" x 3" x 1", **$20**. Patti Polk image, Jason Badgley Collection

◀ Rough exterior of ovoid jasper.
Patti Polk image, Jason Badgley Collection

▶ Ovoid egg
patterns in jasper.
Unique location
discovered by Jason
Badgley, Glendora,
Los Angeles County,
5" x 3" x 2.5", **$40**.
Patti Polk image,
Jason Badgley Collection

California

▲ Iris agate slice in normal light, Acton, Los Angeles County, 2″ x 1.25″ x .12″.
Patti Polk image, Jason Badgley Collection

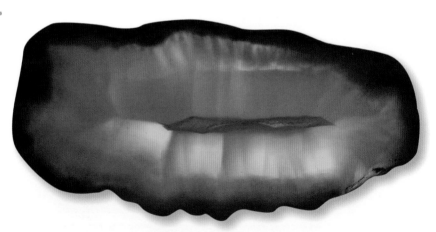

▲ The same agate slice viewed in the proper light to see the Iris effect. **$45**.
Patti Polk image, Jason Badgley Collection

◀ Exterior of petrified palm root. Patti Polk image, Jason Badgley Collection

▲ Petrified palm root. This area is now closed to collecting. Last Chance Canyon, Kern County, 4" x 3" x 1", **$30**.
Patti Polk image, Jason Badgley Collection

▶ Banded agate with parallax and druzy quartz center, Graham Pass, Riverside County, 3" x 2" x 2", **$35**.
Patti Polk Collection

◀ Rough jasper chunk. This area is now closed to collecting. Last Chance Canyon, Kern County, 5.5" x 5" x 2", **$25**. Patti Polk image, Jason Badgley Collection

California

▲ Very rare Mojave Blue agate, Mojave desert, 3" x 1.25" x 1.25", **$50**. Patti Polk Collection

◀ Polished chapinite, Fort Irwin, San Bernardino County, 3" x 3" x 2", **$25**. Patti Polk image, Jason Badgley Collection

▼ Colorful moss jasp-agate, Lavic Siding, San Bernardino County, 4" x 2" x 1.5", **$20**. Patti Polk image, Jason Badgley Collection

▲ Another example of the diverse jasp-agate that can be found at Lavic Siding, San Bernardino County, 6" x 3.5" x .25", **$20**. Patti Polk Collection

California

◀ Exterior of Paisley agate.
Patti Polk image, Jason Badgley Collection

▲ Fortification agate with flame plumes,
Old stock Paisley Agate. This area is closed to
collecting. Riverside County, 3.5" x 1.5" x 3", **$75**.
Patti Polk image, Jason Badgley Collection

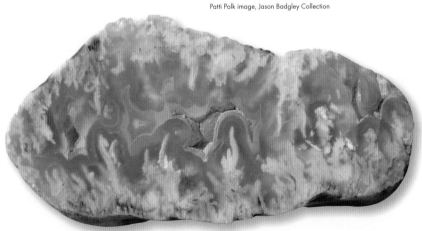

▲ Beach agate with plumes, Malibu, Los Angeles County, 3" x 1.5" x 1", **$35**.
Patti Polk image, Jason Badgley Collection

California

◄ Indian Paint Rock jasper. Closed to collecting. Death Valley, Inyo County, 4.25" x 2.5" x .25", **$15**. Patti Polk Collection

► Rough dendritic agate from Sheep Springs, Randsburg, Kern County, 2.5" x 2" x 1.5", **$10**. Patti Polk Collection

▲ Rough exterior of pisolitic agate. Patti Polk image, Jason Badgley Collection

► Polished pisolitic agate, Ventura, Ventura County, 3.5" x 3" x 2", **$25**. Patti Polk image, Jason Badgley Collection

California

▶ Polished agate with cloud patterns and moss inclusions, Turtle Mountains, San Bernardino County, 3.5" x 2" x 1", **$15**.

Patti Polk image,
Jason Badgley Collection

◀ Polished agate nodule with waterline pattern, Turtle Mountains, San Bernardino County, 3" x 2.5" x 5.5", **$25**.

Patti Polk image,
Jason Badgley Collection

▶ Stone Canyon brecciated jasp-agate slab, San Miguel, San Luis Obispo County, 5" x 3.5" x .25", **$20**.
Patti Polk Collection

◀ Stone Canyon rough brecciated jasp agate, San Miguel, San Luis Obispo County, 3.5" x 2.75" x 2", **$15 per pound**. Patti Polk Collection

▶ Polished petrified wood limb specimen, Boron Dry Lake, Kern County, 3" x 2" x 3.5", **$40**.
Patti Polk image, Jason Badgley Collection

◀ Polished chapinite specimen from an unusual location in Ventura County, 4" x 3" x 2.5", **$35**.
Patti Polk image,
Jason Badgley Collection

California

▶ Exterior view of Lead Pipe Springs thunderegg.
Patti Polk image,
Jason Badgley Collection

▲ Polished blue agate in rhyolite thunderegg, now closed as it is part of Fort Irwin military base. Lead Pipe Springs, San Bernardino County, 3.5" x 3" x 1", **$45**. Patti Polk image, Jason Badgley Collection

◀ Polished slab of agate with marcasite tubes, Nipomo, San Luis Obispo County, 3.5" x 3.5" x .25", **$35**. Patti Polk image, Jason Badgley Collection

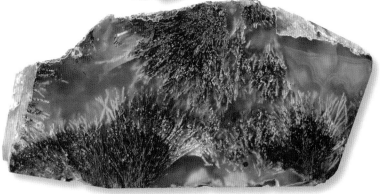

▲ Polished sagenite in agate specimen, Nipomo, San Luis Obispo County, 3" x 1.5" x 2", **$45**.
Patti Polk image, Jason Badgley Collection

◀ Orbicular jasper, Morgan Hill, Santa Clara County, 5" x 3" x 1", **$20**.
Patti Polk image,
Jason Badgley Collection

▲ Brecciated jasper slab, Cayucos, San Luis Obispo County, 7" x 3" x .25", **$18.**
Patti Polk image, Jason Badgley Collection

▲ Polished sagenite specimen, Barstow,
San Bernardino County, 4.5" x 2" x .5",
$50. Patti Polk image, Jason Badgley Collection

▶ Polished banded
agate thunderegg,
Templeton, San Luis
Obispo County,
4" x 3.5" x 3", **$40**.
Patti Polk image, Jason Badgley Collection

◀ Flame agate slab. Location now closed. Bullion Mountains, San Bernardino County, 3″ x 2.5″ x .25″, **$45**. Patti Polk Collection

▲ Agate from Copco, Siskiyou County, 3.5″ x .75″ x 1.5″, **$15**.
Patti Polk image, Jason Badgley Collection

◀ Banded beach agate, Patrick's Point, Humboldt County, 2.25″ x 1.5″ x 1″, **$1**.
Patti Polk image, Jason Badgley Collection

▶ Polished Gelsonite with plume agate specimen, Agoura Hills, Los Angeles County, 3.5" x 1.75" x 1.5", **$55**.
Patti Polk image, Jason Badgley Collection

▶ Agate and opalite in orbicular rhyolite from Opal Mountain, Hinkley, San Bernardino County, 5" x 3" x 4", **$20**.
Patti Polk Collection

▲ Polished cabochon from Opal Mountain cherry opalite, 1" x .5" x .25", **$20**. Patti Polk Collection

▲ Rough orbicular Poppy Jasper, Hornitos, Mariposa County, 3.5" x 3.25" x 1.25", **$30**.
Patti Polk Collection

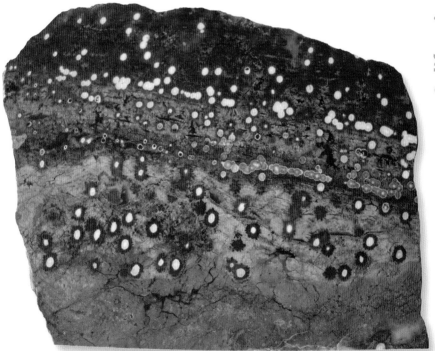

▲ Orbicular Poppy Jasper slab, Hornitos, Mariposa County, 4.25" x 3.25" x 1.25", **$35**.
Patti Polk Collection

► Unusual orbicular jasper for this location, Malibu, Los Angeles County, 3.5" x 2.5" x 1", **$20**. Patti Polk image, Jason Badgley Collection

◄ Polished agate with marcasite inclusions, Malibu, Los Angeles County, 3" x 2.5" x 2", **$45**. Patti Polk image, Jason Badgley Collection

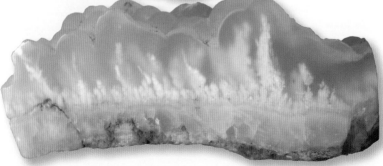

▲ Polished plume agate. This location is now in the middle of a housing development. Encino, Los Angeles County, 2.5" x .75" x 1.25", **$25**. Patti Polk image, Jason Badgley Collection

◀ Wingate Wash plume agate polished slab, Death Valley, Inyo County, **$50**.
Patti Polk image,
Pat McMahan Collection

▶ Agatized fossil whale bone, Jalama Beach, Santa Barbara County, 3" x 2" x 3", **$20**. Patti Polk Collection

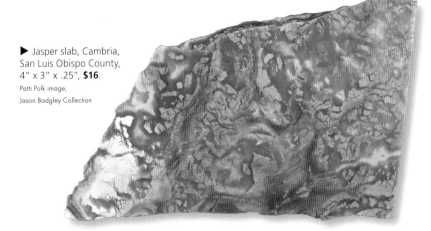

▶ Jasper slab, Cambria, San Luis Obispo County, 4" x 3" x .25", **$16**.
Patti Polk image,
Jason Badgley Collection

California

► Polished banded agate nodule,
Los Olivos, Santa Barbara County,
1.75" x 1.5" x 1", **$20**.

▲ Colorful Rainbow Ridge
jasp-agate rough, Randsburg,
Kern County, 4" x 2.5" x 2",
$10 per pound.

► Cut nodule with
snowflakes and waterline
pattern, Chuckwalla Springs,
Riverside County, 1.25" x 1" x 1.5",
$10.

California

◀ Polished plasma agate slab, Clear Creek, San Benito County, 3″ x 2″ x .25″, **$7 per pound**. Patti Polk Collection

▶ Flame agate slab from the South Cady Mountains, San Bernardino County, 6″ x 3.5″ x .25″, **$50**. Patti Polk Collection

California

◀ Rhyolite geode with well developed quartz crystals in center, Vidal Wash, San Bernardino County, 3″ x 2.5″ x 3″, **$18**. Patti Polk Collection

▲ Polished Edison petrified palm root, Bakersfield, Kern County, 3" x 1.5" x .5", **$25**.
Patti Polk image, Jason Badgley Collection

▲ A colorful Chapinite slab, Chapinite is a brecciated nodular jasper, Siam Siding, San Bernardino County, 5" x 3.5" x .25", **$20**. Patti Polk image, Jason Badgley Collection

Colorado

For more information about rockhounding journeys and what kind of minerals can be found in Colorado, visit www.peaktopeak.com/colorado.

From the Front Range of the Rockies east to Kansas and Nebraska, Colorado consists of high prairie plains, while the central part of the state is composed of the massive and mineral-rich Rocky Mountains. To the west of the Rocky Mountains lies the Colorado Plateau with mesas and plateaus spreading across the state into Utah. It is here, on the Colorado Plateau, that the greatest concentration of agates, jaspers, fossils, and petrified wood can be found, although there are many other agate-collecting locations within other areas of the state. Popular agate-collecting locations in the state include Canon City, Fremont County; Del Norte and Wolf Creek Pass, Rio Grande County; Creede, Mineral County; and El Paso, Elbert, and Weld counties for agate and petrified wood. On the eastern plains, deposits of agate, petrified wood, and fossils can be found over widespread areas.

◀ Rough jasp-agate, Salida, Chaffee County, 4" x 2" x 3", **$15**. Patti Polk image, Jason Badgley Collection

▶ Del Norte biconoid, Rio Grande
County, 3″ x 2″ x 3.5″, **$30**.
Patti Polk image, Jason Badgley Collection

▲ Del Norte plume agate thunderegg, Rio Grande County, 3.5″ x 2.5″ x 2″, **$35**.
Patti Polk image, Jason Badgley Collection

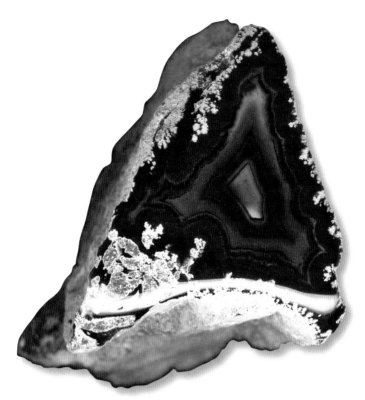

▲ Banded agate nodule from Curecanti, Gunnison County, **$25**. Jeff Anderson Collection

▲ Polished slice of Del Norte plume agate, Rio Grande County, **$40**. Patti Polk image, Pat McMahan Collection

◀ Agatized Hermanophyton Fern fossil, McElmo, Montezuma County, **$100**.
Patti Polk image, Pat McMahan Collection

▶ Petrified wood slab, Castlewood, Arapahoe County. 2" x 1.75" x .25", **$15**. Patti Polk Collection

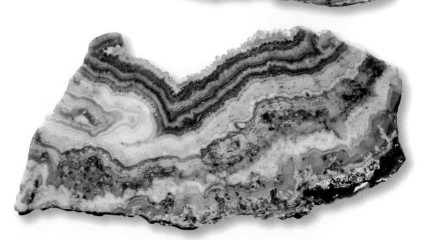

▲ Sowbelly lace agate slab, Creede, Mineral County, 8.5" x 4" x .25", **$25**. Patti Polk Collection

Connecticut

For more information about the preservation
of rocks, minerals, and fossils by the
Connecticut Valley Mineral Club,
visit www.cvmineralclub.org.

This state is bisected by the Connecticut River Valley, creating diverse eastern and western sections. The trap rock of the central valley contains some areas of agate and jasper along with other gem minerals such as quartz and beryl. Reports of agate and jasper as float occur in the following areas: East Granby, Hartford County; East Haven, Milford, Guilford, North Branford and Southbury in New Haven County; Middlefield, Middlesex County; Farmington, Hartford County; Torrington and Woodbury, Litchfield County; and on the beach at Old Saybrook in New London County.

Delaware

For more information about mineralogy, paleontology, and lapidary arts, visit the Delaware Mineralogical Society at www.delminsociety.net.

Delaware consists of two main provinces, the Atlantic Coastal Plain and the Piedmont Province. The coastal plain consists of unconsolidated sediments containing various concentrations of gravels, silt, clay, and sand. The Piedmont formation contains metamorphic and igneous rocks overlaid by the younger coastal sediments, except for the hills of New Castle County, which rise approximately 400 feet above sea level. There are no reports of any known deposits of collectible agates or jaspers in Delaware, although there could always be some scattered occurrences in river gravels.

Florida

For more information about rockhounding in Florida, including a listing of rock and mineral clubs, visit www.freewebs.com/flminerals.

Florida is a long sea-level peninsula with many lakes and southern swamps. The northwest area is mostly hills while the east is coastal plains. Florida is most known for its fossil agatized coral, found in ancient ocean beds where silica rich groundwater has percolated through them and replaced the calcium carbonate skeleton with chalcedony. The fossil coral is approximately 38 to 25 million years old and is from the Oligocene-Miocene period. The coral occurs in a number of colors including black, gray, white, brown, yellow, and red. It is primarily found in the Tampa Bay area, near Ballast Point, Hillsborough County, and to the north on the Withlacoochee River in Madison County, and in Gadsden and Hamilton counties. Chert, agatized coral, and fossils, such as shark teeth, can be found in many river gravels, quarries, and beaches in the counties of Jackson, Levy, Lafayette, Gilchrist, Manatee, Sarasota, Suwanne, Pinella, Pasco, and Polk.

▲ Polished agatized fossil coral, Tampa Bay, Hillsborough County, 4.5" x 2" x .75", **$45**.
Patti Polk image, Jason Badgley Collection

▲ Polished agatized fossil coral,
Withlacoochee River, Madison County,
6" x 2.5" x 2", **$35**. Patti Polk image

▶ Exterior of Withlacoochee
River fossil coral. Patti Polk image

◀ Exterior of Suwanee River fossil coral.
Patti Polk image, Jason Badgley Collection

▲ Agatized fossil coral, Suwanee River, Madison County, 4.5" x 2.5" x 4", **$20**.
Patti Polk image, Jason Badgley Collection

▲ Polished agatized fossil coral, Tampa Bay, Hillsborough County, 4.5" x 3" x 2.5", **$55**.
Patti Polk image, Jason Badgley Collection

▲ Exterior of Tampa bay fossil coral. Patti Polk image, Jason Badgley Collection

Georgia

To learn more about rocks, gems and minerals in Georgia, visit the Georgia Mineral Society, Inc. at www.gamineral.org.

Georgia exhibits rock from almost every geologic period. Sedimentary rocks underlie the low coastal plain in the southern half of the state, while middle Georgia contains the Piedmont Plateau. In the upper northeast corner resides a highland area rich in crystalline minerals. The northwest corner is eroded and folded ancient sedimentary rock. Collecting locations include areas for chert, agate, and agatized fossil coral. Red jasper may be found in Flint River gravels, Dougherty County; Savannah River agate can be found near Girard, Burke County; petrified wood near Bull and Randall Creeks, Muscogee County; agate near Summerville, Chattooga County; Meriwether County; and agatized coral on the Withlacoochee River, Lowndes county. Red oolitic jasper occurs near Tarr Creek in Whitfield County, and varying amounts of agate, chert, opalite, petrified wood, and jasper can be found in Bartow, Bibb, Chattahoochee, Cobb, Crisp, Hancock, Screven, and Walker counties.

▶ Polished lace agate cabochon, Summerville, Chattooga County, 25mm long, **$15**. Mike Streeter Collection

◀ Lacy banded agate, Summerville, Chattooga County, 3" x 2" x 1.5", **$20**.
Patti Polk Collection

◀ Rough exterior of fossil coral.
Patti Polk image, Jason Badgley Collection

▶ Agatized fossil coral, Withlacoochee River, Lowndes County, 4" x 4" x 3", **$35**. Patti Polk image, Jason Badgley Collection

Georgia

Georgia

▶ Savannah
River agate,
$3 per pound.
Mike Streeter Collection

▲ Savannah River agate,
$3 per pound. Mike Streeter Collection

▶ Polished agatized coral cabochon,
Lowndes County, 40mm long, **$45**.
Mike Streeter Collection

▲ Agatized coral from Lowndes County,
$5 per pound. Mike Streeter Collection

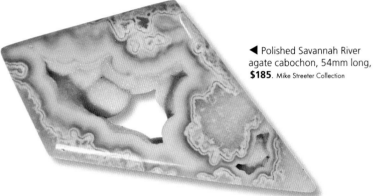

◀ Polished Savannah River
agate cabochon, 54mm long,
$185. Mike Streeter Collection

Georgia

▶ Agatized coral from
Lowndes County,
$3 per pound.
Mike Streeter Collection

▲ Water-worn agatized fossil coral, Withlacoochee River, Lowndes County, 5.5" 3" x 2", **$35**.
Patti Polk image, Jason Badgley Collection

▲ Exterior of fossil coral, Withlacoochee River. Patti Polk image, Jason Badgley Collection

Hawaii

For more information about mineral and rock collecting, visit the Rock & Mineral Society of Hawaii at pohakugalore.net/Hui_pohaku/Hiu_pohaku_1.html.

Although Hawaii isn't located on the North American continent, it is a part of the United States and has a few minor agate locations, so I am including it here for reference purposes. The Hawaiian Islands are formed of volcanic basaltic lava eroded into valleys and mountains, but the comparatively recent volcanic activity and topography makes agate formation very unlikely. For agate collectors, the island of Oahu is the only known Hawaiian location where you can find agates and jaspers. Jasper can be found on the north shore of Kailua in basalt ridges and ravines from Mount Olokanu, in the washes of the Keolu Hills, and in the H & D quarry. In the Wahiawa Valley, jasper can be found in the washes of the Lanikai golf course. In Kaneohe, jasper can be found on ridges in the Koolau range, and at Olomana Peak, banded agate can be found in gullies and in the crater of the West Molokai volcano.

Idaho

For more information about rockhounding, visit the Idaho Department of Lands at www.idl.idaho.gov/bureau/minerals/ gem_guide/gg_index.htm.

Idaho is rich in mineral resources and diverse in geographical topography. The rugged mountain ranges in the northern and central regions contain many rivers and lakes, and the basaltic Columbia Lava Plateau connects with Oregon and Washington, covering many square miles in the northern area of the state. Southern Idaho is fairly arid sagebrush desert, and holds many famous agate and jasper collecting locations. In western and southwestern Idaho, occur the well-known Owyhee and Bruneau jasper deposits, and the Graveyard Point plume agate on the Oregon/Idaho border. Petrified wood, opals, and fossils may also be found in Idaho. Precious opal may be mined for a fee at the Spencer Opal Mine near the town of Spencer in Clark County. Agates, jaspers, and petrified wood can be found in Custer, Owyhee, Blaine, Lemhi, Gem, Washington, Gooding, Idaho, Lincoln, Nez Perce, and Ada counties.

◀ Bruneau jasper rough, Bruneau, Owyhee County, 1.75" x 1.25" x 1.5", **$25 per pound**. Patti Polk image, Jason Badgley Collection

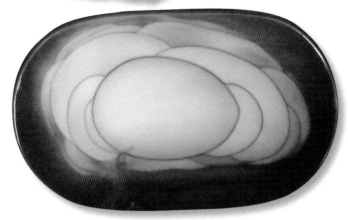

▲ Polished Bruneau jasper specimen showing egg patterns, Bruneau, Owyhee County, **$60**. Patti Polk image, Pat McMahan Collection

◀ Polished sagenite agate nodule, Hog Creek, Washington County, **$45**. Patti Polk image, Pat McMahan Collection

Idaho

▲ Moss jasp-agate slab, Hog Creek,
Washington County, 10" x 4" x .25",
$25. Patti Polk image, Rimrock Gems Collection

◀ Road Creek banded agate,
Challis, Custer County, **$30**.
Jeff Anderson Collection

Idaho

▲ Waterline agate slab with moss inclusions, Hellsgate, Nez Perce County, 4.5" x 2" x .25", **$15**.
Patti Polk Collection

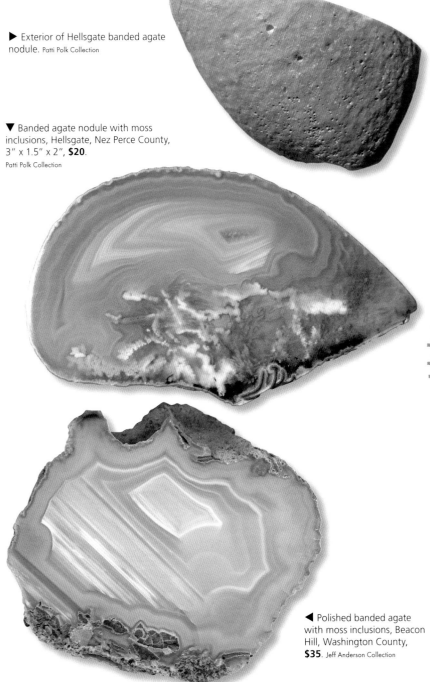

▶ Exterior of Hellsgate banded agate nodule. Patti Polk Collection

▼ Banded agate nodule with moss inclusions, Hellsgate, Nez Perce County, 3″ x 1.5″ x 2″, **$20**.
Patti Polk Collection

◀ Polished banded agate with moss inclusions, Beacon Hill, Washington County, **$35**. Jeff Anderson Collection

Idaho

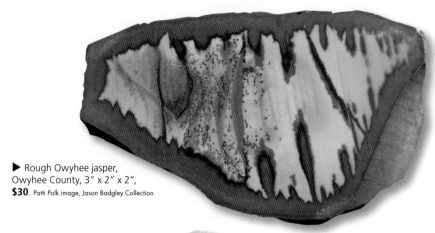

► Rough Owyhee jasper,
Owyhee County, 3" x 2" x 2",
$30. Patti Polk image, Jason Badgley Collection

◄ Waterline agate
nodule with quartz
crystals, Beacon Hill,
Washington County,
1.5" x 1.25" x 1",
$38 per pound.
Patti Polk Collection

▲ Willow Creek porcelain jasper with egg patterns, Boise,
Ada County, 4" x 1.75" x 2.5", **$10**. Patti Polk image, Jason Badgley Collection

▲ Rough Graveyard Point plume agate, Homedale, Owyhee County, 4″ x 3″ x 6″, **$10 per pound**. Patti Polk Collection

◄ Graveyard Point plume agate slab, Homedale, Owyhee County, 3″ x 2.5″ x .25″, **$10 per pound**. Patti Polk Collection

▶ Wild Horse picture jasper slab, Owyhee County, 3" x 2.5" x .25", **$4.50 per pound**.
Patti Polk Collection

▲ Polished Spiderweb jasper cabochon, Owyhee County, 1.5" x 1.25" x .25", **$30.**
Patti Polk image, Jason Badgley Collection

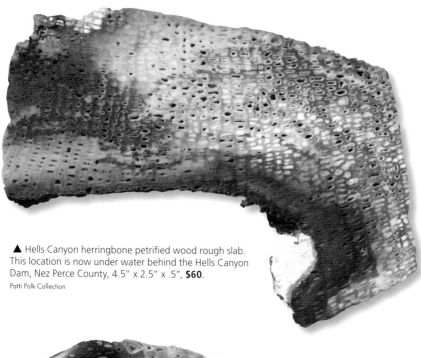

▲ Hells Canyon herringbone petrified wood rough slab.
This location is now under water behind the Hells Canyon
Dam, Nez Perce County, 4.5" x 2.5" x .5", **$60**.
Patti Polk Collection

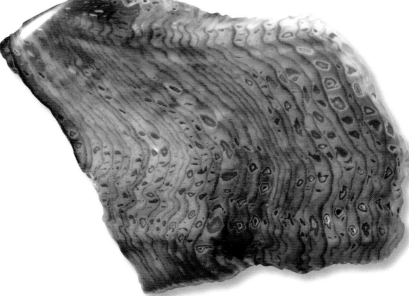

▲ Rare piece of polished herringbone pattern petrified wood. The small holes were created by dry
rot before the trees were petrified and then later filled with minerals that coated their walls with
tiny crystals like miniature geodes. Hells Canyon Reservoir, Nez Perce County, 2.25" x 1.5" x .25",
$50. Patti Polk Collection

Idaho

▲ Prudent Man plume/flame agate slab, Arco, Butte County, 9" x 3" x .25", **$18**.
Patti Polk image, Rimrock Gems Collection

▲ Polished sagenite agate nodule, Hellsgate, Nez Perce County, **$25**. Jeff Anderson Collection

Iowa

For more information about mineralogy, geology and gemology, visit Cedar Valley Rocks & Minerals Society at cedarvalleyrockclub.org.

Most of Iowa is a prairie tableland of glacial moraine resting on sedimentary rocks. Only the far northeastern corner escaped the glacier's impact and is comprised of low hills and cliffs. In the extreme west, dome shaped bluffs rise from the Missouri river's floodplain. Iowa ranks high in the production of clay, limestone, gravel, and sand, due to the fact that it was under ocean waters through the Mesozoic era. The Devonian period limestone produces wonderful agatized fossil corals and stromatopariods, while chert and geodes erode from the sedimentary rock. Lake Superior agates can be collected in many eastern areas of the state, especially along the Mississippi River in the river gravels and at commercial quarries. Petrified wood can also be found in many of the river gravels. Keswick agate may be found in Keswick quarry, Keokuk County, and Coldwater agate can be found in Benton, Black Hawk, Bremer, Delaware, Linn, and Keokuk counties. Nicely banded chert occurs in limestone formations near Mount Pleasant in Henry County, and quartz geodes are found in the vicinity of Keokuk in Lee County.

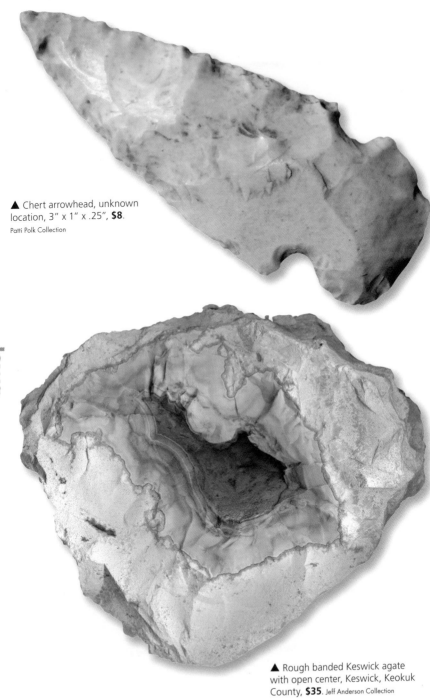

▲ Chert arrowhead, unknown
location, 3" x 1" x .25", **$8**.
Patti Polk Collection

▲ Rough banded Keswick agate
with open center, Keswick, Keokuk
County, **$35**. Jeff Anderson Collection

▶ Water-worn Lake Superior agate from the Cedar River gravels, Muscatine County, **$15 per pound**.
Jeff Anderson Collection

▲ Lacy fortification Keswick agate, Keokuk County, **$45**. Teyet Kepling Collection

Iowa

Illinois

For more information about
rockhounding events, visit the
Chicago Rocks and Minerals Society
at www.chicagorocks.org.

The Prairie State is underlain with sedimentary rocks containing silica sand, oil, coal, and sandstone buried by glacial sand and gravels. A wide variety of fossils are found in the Upper Carboniferous systems of altered sandstone, shale, bituminous slates, limestone, and seams of coal in Will, Vermilion, Randolph, Henderson, Hancock, Grundy, and Fulton counties. Quartz geodes from the Warsaw Formation are also commonly found in Illinois, and more uncommon chalcedony-lined geodes have been found in Monroe, Calhoun, and Hancock counties. Agates and jaspers are found in Alexander, Henry, Pulaski, and Vermilion counties. Water-worn agates can be found in river gravels in Hancock County.

▶ "White Ringer"
agate with quartz
center from Jacob's
Quarry, Hamilton,
Hancock County,
$35. Jeff Anderson Collection

◀ Banded agate with open center from Warsaw area, Hancock County, **$35**. Jeff Anderson Collection

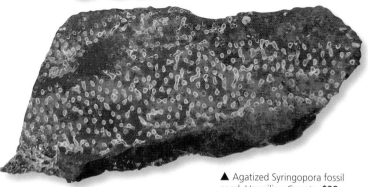

▲ Agatized Syringopora fossil coral, Vermilion County, **$28**.
Teyet Kepling Collection

◀ Fossilized Brachiopod jasper, Vermilion County, **$35**. Teyet Kepling Collection

Illinois

▲ Scenic jasper,
Vermilion County, **$20**.
Teyet Kepling Collection

▲ Fortification agate nodule, Vermilion County, **$35**. Teyet Kepling Collection

▲ Agatized Favosites fossil coral, Vermilion County, **$28**. Teyet Kepling Collection

▲ Moss agate, Vermilion County, **$18**. Teyet Kepling Collection

Illinois

▲ Lacy moss agate, Vermilion County, **$45**.
Teyet Kepling Collection

▲ Glacially deposited petrified wood, Vermilion County, **$22**. Teyet Kepling Collection

▲ Petrified Psaronius fern wood, Vermilion County, **$25**. Teyet Kepling Collection

▲ Exterior of petrified Psaronius fern wood, Salt Fork River, Vermilion County. Teyet Kepling Collection

Illinois

Indiana

For more information on rock, mineral, fossil, and gem collecting in Indiana, visit the Lawrence County Rock Club at www.lawrencecountyrockclub.org.

Northern Indiana has been smoothed by ancient glaciers that brought detrial moraines from the far north, and contains most of the silicated materials that occur here. The southern half of the state is characterized by bottomlands containing valleys, gorges, and ridges. The geologic formations of Indiana are predominantly sedimentary of Ordovician to Pennsylvanian age, with many Silurian exposures cropping up both east and west across the state in the Newton and Adams counties. The oldest formations occur in the eastern counties, with the youngest rocks appearing in the northeastern and southwestern corners of the state. The most notable formation is the Mississinewa shale, where quantities of fossils may be found. There are no noteworthy igneous rock outcrops in Indiana, and most of the agates and jaspers are found in river gravels. Allen, Brown, Dearborn, Lawrence, and Miami are just a few of the counties where agate, jasper, fossils, and petrified wood occur. Geodes are found in Lawrence and Washington counties.

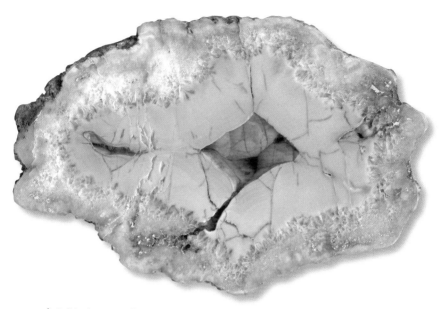

▲ Polished agate and quartz geode, Bedford, Lawrence County, **$35**. Jeff Anderson Collection

▲ Well-agatized marine fossil, 4" x 3" x 2.5". Jefferson County, **$20**. Patti Polk Collection

Kansas

For more information on mineralogy, visit Olathe Shawnee-Mission Gem and Mineral Society at www.gemandmineralclub.org.

The surface of Kansas is mainly open plains covered with sand and gravel derived from erosion of the Rockies that were deposited by water, and is underlain by widespread sedimentary rock. These deposits create eastward sloping high plains where agates and quartz minerals can be found. The sediment beds are filled with coal, salt, and fossils. To the east of the Colorado High Plains are the Smoky Hills and Great Bend Prairie in the north. The Flint Hills run north to south across the state and in the northeast corner is a glaciated region. Western Kansas contains many creeks, streambeds and sand hills that offer agate, jasper, chert, chalcedony, petrified wood, and fossils especially in the counties of Gove, Logan, Trego, and Wallace. In the widespread Ogallala formation encompassing the counties of Clark, Ellis, Logan, Ness, Rawlins, and Wallace, are found deposits of dendritic opal, massive or nodular translucent opal, opalized bones, and petrified wood. Colorful chert can be collected in the Cretaceous chalk beds in Cherokee, Logan, Norton, and Phillips counties.

▲ Moss dendritic opalite, Logan County, 1.25" x 1" x 1.5", **$5**. Patti Polk Collection

▲ Lake Superior river polished agate, McLouth, Jefferson County, 1″ x 1″ x 1″, **$15 per pound**.
Patti Polk Collection

▲ Dendritic opalite, Quinter, Gove County, 3″ x 1.75″ x 4″, **$15**.
Patti Polk image, Jason Badgley Collection

Kentucky

The Kentucky Geological Survey at www.uky.edu/KGS/rocksmn has more information about rocks and minerals, and a list of clubs.

Kentucky is primarily a sedimentary-based state, and contains part of the Mississippian plateau in the south and southwest where there are extensive coalfields. In eastern Kentucky, still more coalfields abound in the rough terrain of the Allegheny plateau. In the north are the rolling hills of bluegrass country. Kentucky is part of a very old land surface, lying within the eastern uplifted Appalachian Plateau and the westerly Interior Low Plateaus. During most of the Paleozoic and Mesozoic eras, Kentucky lay beneath the sea, and its rock formations are predominantly sedimentary shales, sandstones, and limestone with very little igneous or metamorphic intrusions. Outcropping rocks in this region containfew collectable gemstones but great

▲ Chert knife tool from Kentucky, 2.5" x 1.25", **$18**. Patti Polk Collection

amounts of fossils. Often, wherever the Fort Payne and Warsaw formations of the Mississippian Period appear, geodes can be found in good numbers. Nodules can be found in many sizes from small to larger than fist-sized and some contain beautifully banded chalcedony, while others have interiors lined with crystals of calcite, celestite, fluorite, goethite, pryrite, and quartz. Throughout the Warsaw formation, the investigation of creeks, streambeds and banks, road cuts, and other excavations almost always reveal a generous supply of geodes. The counties of Adair, Allen, Barren, Hardin, Lincoln, Lyon, Madison, and Monroe are all good bets for finding geodes. Beautifully colored fortification agate concretionary nodules occur in Estill, Powell, and Jackson counties. Fossil coral and petrified wood can be found in Jefferson County; agate, chert, jasper, and petrified wood pebbles are found in gravel pits in Graves County, and chert, jasper, oolites, and fossils can be found in Rockcastle and Rowan counties.

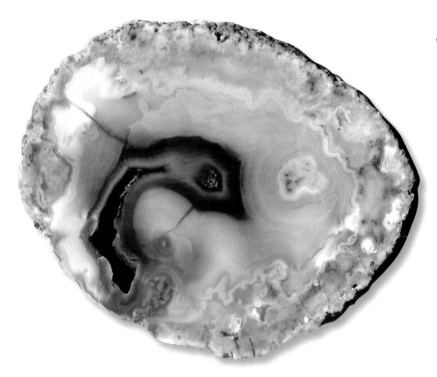

Kentucky

▲ Agate nodule with black band around center cavity, Borden Formation, Estill County, 3.5″ x 2.5″ x 2″, **$45**. Patti Polk image, Jason Badgley Collection

▲ Red, yellow and blue/grey banded agate nodule, Borden Formation, Estill County, **$45**.
Jeff Anderson Collection

▲ Colorful multi-band fortification agate nodule, Borden Formation, Estill County, **$60**.
Jeff Anderson Collection

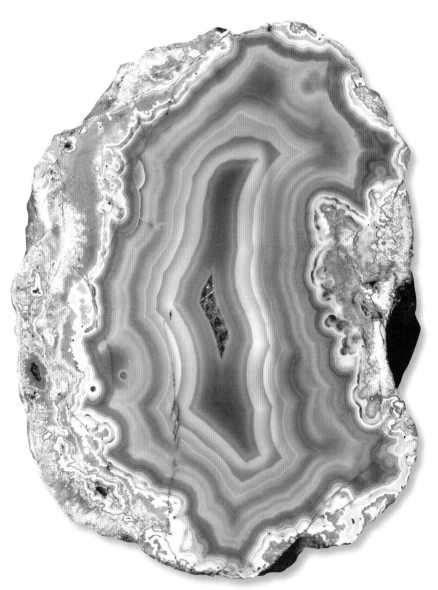

▲ Banded agate nodule, Borden Formation, Estill County, **$70**. Jeff Anderson Collection

Louisiana

The Ark-La-Tex Gem & Mineral Society promotes earth sciences, the art of lapidaries and their related fields. For more information, visit www.larockclub.com.

The Mississippi River has dominated and formed the state into what we see today by depositing mud and sand carried down from the north for millennia. To the west of the river lie alluvial plains and low hills that contain gravel deposits where agates can be found. Collecting sites include the Harrison, Livingston, Tangipahoa, Ouachita, Rapides, and Vernon counties where the many streams and riverbeds collect petrified wood, agate, jasper, palm and petrified coral. Tertiary formations outcrop in nearly every parish to yield petrified wood (mostly hickory, oak, poplar and palm), and large silicified logs have been found in the De Sota Parish. Banded agate and opalized wood can be found in the gravels of the Ouachita River in Ouachita Parish.

▲ Mississippi River banded agate in gravels, Feliciana Parish, 3" x 2" x 1", **$15**. Patti Polk Collection

▲ Petrified palm limb, Sabine Parish,
6.5" x 3" x 4.5", **$40**. Patti Polk Collection

Louisiana

▲ Petrified palm slab, Sabine Parish, 6" x 5" x .25", **$25**. Patti Polk Collection

Maine

The Maine Mineralogical & Geological Society is dedicated to geology, mineralogy, lapidary arts and related subjects. For more information, visit mainemineralclub.org.

Eroded to bedrock by thick Pleistocene glaciers, Maine lays on a foundation of sandstone, limestone and shale. As the glaciers receded, they left deposits of basal sediments that dammed the valleys and created some 2,200 lakes and over 5,000 rivers and streams where collecting in gravel beds is possible. Maine is best known for its splendid tourmalines and other gemstones, but there are a few locations where agates and jaspers can be found. Jasper can be found in the Swift River in Oxford County, and agate and jasper can be found on the beaches near Perry in Washington County.

▲ Large banded beach agate, Perry, Washington County, 4" x 3.5" x 1.75", **$5**.
Lance Shope Collection

▶ Fortification-type beach agate, Perry, Washington County, 2″ x 1.5″ x 1.5″, **$5**. Lance Shope Collection

◀ Close up of a lacy, lattice agate, Perry, Washington County.
Lance Shope Collection

▶ Face polished carnelian slab, Perry, Washington County, 1.5″ x 1″ x 1.5″, **$20**.
Lance Shope Collection

◀ Banded jasp-agate slab, Perry, Washington County, **$15**. Lance Shope Collection

Maine

▶ Jasp-agate, Perry, Washington County, 3" x 2" x 2.75", **$20**. Lance Shope Collection

◀ Brightly banded fortification agate, Perry, Washington County, 2.25" x 1.5" x 1", **$20**.
Lance Shope Collection

▶ Rough exterior of lattice agate, Perry, Washington County, **$25**.
Lance Shope Collection

◀ Lace agate slab, Perry, Washington County, 3.5" x 2" x .25", **$15**. Lance Shope Collection

Maine

Maryland

For a listing of fossil, rock, gem and mineral clubs and societies, visit the Maryland Geological Survey site at www.mgs.md.gov/esic/fs/fs14.html.

Divided by the Chesapeake Bay, Maryland is characterized by three different geological provinces. The flat Coastal Plain extends westward from the present margin of the continental shelf to the Fall Line, underlain by unconsolidated clays, sands, and gravels dipping at a low angle toward the southeast. The Piedmont Plateau forms the central part of Maryland, extending westward from the plains to the east side of South Mountain. In the west and north, the Piedmont rises to the Blue Ridge and hills of Pennsylvania. The Appalachian Province spans the region between South Mountain and the West Virginia border. In the extreme southwestern corner of Garrett Co., almost on the West Virginia line, rises the highest point in Maryland, Backbone Mountain. Jasper and chalcedony occur in Baltimore, Frederick (Point of Rock), Harford, and Montgomery counties, and moss agate has been found in the hills near Flintville in Harford County. You can find petrified wood in streams in Prince Georges County and Calvert County has fossils and shark teeth on the shores of the Chesapeake Bay.

Massachusetts

The Boston Mineral Club promotes studying and collecting rocks and minerals, and offers educational programs and field trips. For more information, visit www.bostonmineralclub.org.

The Connecticut River divides the state into two main geographical areas. In the east are coastal plains underlain with metamorphic schists marked with many lakes and rapid, short rivers. To the west, uplands rise toward the Berkshire Hills and the Appalachian Mountains. Jasper, agate and chalcedony can be found in the counties of Barnstable, Essex, Franklin, Hampden, Hampshire, Northfolk, and Plymouth. Although these are mainly found as beach pebbles, there have been reports of agates in nodule form near Deerfield in Franklin County.

Michigan

The Michigan Mineralogical Society
furthers the hobby of minerals, fossils,
gem collecting, geology and earth science
education. For more information,
visit www.michmin.org.

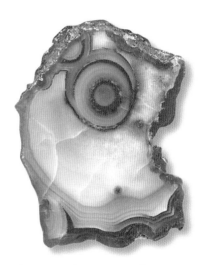

▲ Copper replacement agate from
Kearsage Lobe, Houghton County, **$100**.
Jeff Anderson Collection

Michigan is separated into two distinct parts by the Ice Age waters of Lake Michigan. Upper Michigan is a rugged land made of igneous and metamorphic rock containing many of the richest copper and iron deposits in the world. Most of southern Michigan is fairly level and only slightly elevated above the Great Lakes, and contains sedimentary deposits of salt, limestone and gypsum. The agate collector will find that there are two different types of collecting to be done in Michigan — hunting along the state's lake beaches for Lake Superior agates or working over almost countless iron and copper mine dumps for copper-included agates and jaspers. The water-worn Lake Superior agates are generally fairly small but beautifully banded and quite colorful in shades of red, white, pink, and brown. Although technically not an agate, datolite, a mineral that forms as a porcelain-type nodule colored by copper specific to this location, is found in the copper mines of the Upper Peninsula. Datolites can be found in Houghton, Keweenaw, and Ontonagon counties. Agate, jasper, chalcedony, chert, and fossil coral can be found in the counties of Alpena, Chippewa, Clinton, Houghton, Keweenaw, Livingston, Luce, Oakland, Ontonagon, and Marquette counties.

▲ Brockway Mountain agate from Copper Harbor, Keweenaw County, **$20**. Jeff Anderson Collection

▲ Underwater agate collected along Lake Superior shoreline at Keweenaw Point, **$15 per pound**. Jeff Anderson Collection

▶ Lake Superior beach agate, Two Heart River, Luce County, **$15 per pound**. Jeff Anderson Collection

◀ Well agatized fossil coral, also known as Petosky Stone, Emmet County. 3.5" x 2" x 3", **$15**. Patti Polk Collection

▶ Polished Iron Lace agate from the New Republic Iron Mine, Marquette County, **$55**. Jeff Anderson Collection

◀ Unusually colored banded Lake Superior beach agate, 1.5″ x 1.25 x 2″, **$15 per pound**.
Patti Polk Collection

▼ Copper in jasper slab, Keweenaw Peninsula, 4.5″ x 4″ x .25″, **$40**.
Patti Polk Collection

◀ Copper replacement agate, Houghton County, 1.5″ x 1.25″ x .75″, **$35**.
Patti Polk Collection

▲ Exterior of datolite nodule.
Patti Polk Collection

◀ Porcelain pink datolite nodule, Caledonia Mine, Ontonagon County, 1.5″ x 1.5″ x .75″, **$65**. Patti Polk Collection

Michigan

Minnesota

For more information about mineralogy, geology, paleontology and the lapidary arts, visit The Minnesota Mineral Club at www.minnesotamineralclub.org.

This nearly level state is a broad glaciated plain with an elevation of 1,000 to 1,500 feet above sea level. Immense deposits of glacial drift, consisting of gravels, sands, and clays dominate the state's surface topography. The only section that might be termed at all mountainous lies in the northeastern triangle of the state. Here the Lake Superior hill ranges (Sawteeth, Mesabi, Cuyuna, Gunflint, Giant's Range, and Vermillion) expose a few eroded and rounded peaks nearly 2,000 feet above sea level.

By far the most widely distributed and popular gemstone for which Minnesota is noted is the Lake Superior agate, distinguished by its hardness, rich colors, variety, and fine parallel banding. Lake Superior agates are usually found in sizes from 1/2-2 inches in diameter (with an occasional nodule weighing several pounds) and often considered to be one of the most desirable agates to collect in the U.S.A. A few of the most recognizable forms include eye agates, sagenite included agates, an onyx-like banded agate, and fortification agate. Practically every glacial moraine of drift deposit, gravel bank and stream bar, lake beach, quarry, excavation, and gravel pit in the entire state yields up a surprising abundance of this eagerly sought after gemstone.

Other collectible materials in Minnesota include Mary Ellen jasper, a fossil stromatolite from St. Louis County, and Binghamite, a silicified iron material from Crow Wing County.

Jasper, Lake Superior and other agates can be found in Carlton, Cook, Crow Wing, Hennepin, Lake, Olmsted, St. Louis, Wabasha, and Winona counties.

◀ Polished Lake Superior banded agate, 1.75" x 1.25" x 1.25", **$15 per pound**.
Patti Polk Collection

▶ "Binghamite," a chatoyant jasper included with fibrous goethite from the Cuyuna Iron Range, Crow Wing County, 3" x 2" x 3", **$12 per pound**.
Patti Polk Collection

◀ Tumble polished Lake Superior banded agate with quartz center, 1.25" x 1" x 1", **$15 per pound**.
Patti Polk Collection

▶ Rough Lake Superior banded agate, 1" x 1" x 1.5", **$15 per pound**. Patti Polk Collection

◀ "Mary Ellen" fossil stromatolite jasper slab from the Mesabi Iron Range, St. Louis County, 4" x 3" x .25", **$25**. Patti Polk image, Jason Badgley Collection

Mississippi

For more information about the rock-collecting hobby in this state, visit North Mississippi Gem and Mineral Society at www.nmgms.org.

Like other adjoining states that also lie beneath the ancient extended Gulf of Mexico, all of the state's formations were laid down under salt water as the gulf slowly receded southward from its northern-most reaches below the present Ohio River Valley. Such sedimentation is still going on, wherever rivers discharge their mud, silt, and sand into the Gulf of Mexico.

Few gemstone localities exist in Mississippi, but the state yields an abundance of fossils of many geologic ages. Petrifications occur in the northeastern and central counties, where the preservations occur in iron oxide. Considerable quantities of petrified wood weather out of exposures of the widespread Lafayette formation, with smaller quantities occurring in the Wilcox and other tertiary sediments. A considerable petrified forest area, once noted for its abundance of fossil logs that reached up to 6 feet in diameter, occurs in Madison County. Lake Superior and other agates occur in the river gravels, with jasper, chalcedony and petrified wood (including palm) that can be found in the Adams, Claiborne, Copiah, Harrison, Stone, Wayne, and Yazoo counties.

▲ Mississippi River gravels agate, 1.25" x 1" x 2.5", **$15**.
Patti Polk image, Jason Badgley Collection

► Mississippi River agate, Adams County, 2″ x 1″ x 1.5″, **$4**. Patti Polk Collection

▲ Lake Superior agate from river gravels, Natchez, Adams County, 1.5″ x 1″ x 1″, **$15 per pound**. Patti Polk Collection

Missouri

For more information about the
rock collecting hobby in this state, visit
North Mississippi Gem and Mineral Society
at www.nmgms.org.

The state is dominated by two main rivers, the Mississippi on the eastern border and the Missouri that runs east and south. In the northern part of the state are fertile plains formed by glaciers leaving sedimentary deposits. In the southwest are rolling plains that rise to the Ozark Plateau. There are many coal deposits throughout the state created from the Cretaceous period's marshland and swamps, while epicontinental seas left limestone and sand sediments. A considerable variety of agates and jaspers occur in Missouri. Typical Lake Superior agates are abundant in the glacial drift deposits of Gentry, Davies, Grundy, and Livingston counties, along with agatized coral and bone, chalcedony, jasper, and petrified wood. All along the Mississippi River, gravel operations yield an almost endless supply of fine, high-quality agates and

other collectible gemstones. In Clark County near Kahoka, exposures of the Warsaw formation disgorge good quantities of geodes for the collector.

Agates are most abundant in the glacial and stream

▲ Mozarkite slab, a mix of chert, flint, and jasper, Farmington, St. Francois County, 3.5" x 3" x .25", **$5 per pound**. Patti Polk Collection

gravels in the northern part of the state, and the large gravel pit near LaGrange in the northeast has furnished many beautiful specimens of agate, petrified wood, and fossils.

Chert occurs in much of the southern half of the state and is one of the main sources of gravel in Missouri. In the counties of Benton and Hickory occurs a colorful, cutting-quality chert called Mozarkite, along with chert from McDonald County that is also considered lapidary quality. A unique occurrence of a beautiful concretionary nodule containing fine fortification patterns, called Union Road agate, was discovered near St. Louis during the construction of Interstate Highways 270 and 55, and is now unfortunately covered by business developments.

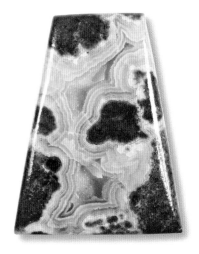

▲ Polished Missouri Lace cabochon, Washington County, 42mm long, **$15**. Mike Streeter Collection

▲ Missouri Lace agate, Washington County, **$35**. Jeff Anderson Collection

▶ Missouri Lace agate slab, Washington County, 3" x 2" x .25", **$18**. Patti Polk Collection

Missouri

▲ Rough chert, Dade County, **$5**. Talequah Club image, Patti Polk Collection

▶ Rough Lake Superior agate from river gravels, Lewis County, 1.5" x 1.25" x 2", **$15 per pound**.
Patti Polk Collection

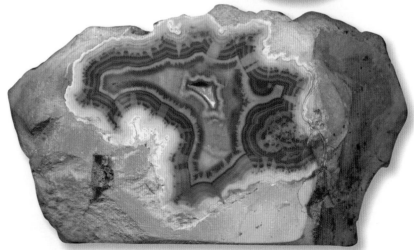

▲ Union Road fortification agate. These are concretionary nodules that formed in a sedimentary environment and are now pretty much buried by civilization. St. Louis, St. Louis County, **$40**.
Jeff Anderson Collection

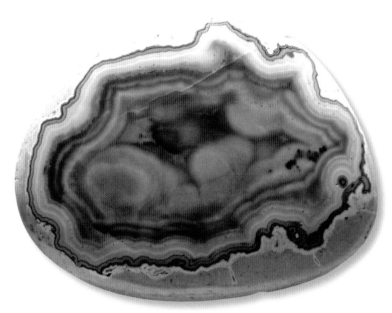

▲ Polished Union Road fortification agate with internal botryoidal pattern, St. Louis, St. Louis County, 2.5" x 2" x 1", **$35**. Patti Polk image, Jason Badgley Collection

▲ Polished Union Road fortification agate with quartz center pocket and border, St. Louis, St. Louis County, 3.5" x 3.25" x 1.25", **$45**. Patti Polk image, Jason Badgley Collection

Montana

For more information about rock-collecting sites, visit the Montana Official State Travel Site, visitmt.com, and type in "rock hounding" in the search.

The Rocky Mountains cross the state from northwest to southeast. In the east are high plains broken by gullies, bluffs, and isolated mountains. Western and southwestern Montana has the Continental Divide that lies under the Bitterroot Range that is the state's western boundary.

Montana is famous for its moss agate, which is a clear to gray chalcedony containing moss and dendritic inclusions that can be found in the gravel bars and adjoining benches along the Yellowstone River and its tributaries for some 250 miles. The agate is widely distributed and can also be found in the fields, valleys, and ranchlands around the state. When sliced, the nodules reveal delicate landscape scenes of mountains, forests, trees, bushes, lakes, and figures. Some Montana moss agates will exhibit the rainbow iris effect when cut properly. Besides the moss agate, Montana has many fine collectible agate, jasper, petrified wood, and fossil locations. Dryhead agate, a beautiful fortification-type agate, comes from southern Montana in Big Horn and Carbon counties near the Wyoming border, and is a highly desirable agate for many collectors.

Agate, chalcedony, jasper, petrified and opalized wood, and fossils can be found in many counties throughout the state, including but not limited to, Beaverhead, Big Horn, Cascade, Custer, Dawson, Gallatin, Lewis and Clark, Madison, Park, Prairie, Silver Bow and Yellowstone counties.

◀ Typical scenic moss agate from the Yellowstone River gravels, 2.5" x 1.5" x 1.5", **$6 per pound**.

Patti Polk image, Jason Badgley Collection

▶ Polished river gravel agate with moss and waterline patterns, 3" x 2.5 x 1.5", **$10 per pound**.

Patti Polk Collection

◀ Polished Dryhead fortification agate nodule, Big Horn and Pryor Mountain Ranges, Carbon County, **$95**. Jeff Anderson Collection

▶ Polished Dryhead fortification agate nodule, Big Horn and Pryor Mountain Ranges, Carbon County, **$125**.

Grant Curtis Collection

Montana

► Polished Dryhead fortification agate nodule, Big Horn and Pryor Mountain Ranges, Carbon County, 4" x 3" x 2", **$50**. Patti Polk image, Jason Badgley Collection

◄ Close-up detail of the Dryhead agate fortification banding. Tom Shearer Collection

Montana

► Fortification agate from Bear Canyon, Pryor Mountains, Carbon County, **$65**. Lowell Foster Collection

◄ Agate with quartz crystal from Bear Canyon, Pryor Mountains, Carbon County, **$50**. Lowell Foster Collection

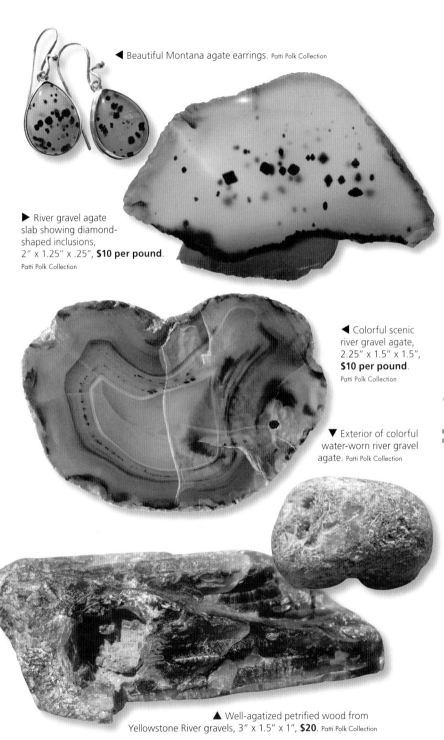

◀ Beautiful Montana agate earrings. Patti Polk Collection

▶ River gravel agate slab showing diamond-shaped inclusions, 2" x 1.25" x .25", **$10 per pound**. Patti Polk Collection

◀ Colorful scenic river gravel agate, 2.25" x 1.5" x 1.5", **$10 per pound**. Patti Polk Collection

▼ Exterior of colorful water-worn river gravel agate. Patti Polk Collection

▲ Well-agatized petrified wood from Yellowstone River gravels, 3" x 1.5" x 1", **$20**. Patti Polk Collection

Montana

Nebraska

For more information about collecting rocks, gems, minerals and fossils in Nebraska, visit the Nebraska Gem and Mineral Club at www.nerockgem.org.

This Great Plains state starts in the northwest at an elevation of 840 feet and slowly rises to 5,300 feet in the southeast. The subsurface rock strata of the entire state is undisturbed sedimentary sandstone, limestone, shale, and clay, with the oldest formation lying in the southeastern corner.

Northwestern Nebraska contains many of the gem fields in the state because both the Black Hills of South Dakota and the Badlands have long spurs that run into this part of the state. In this rough region you can find Fairburn agates, fluorescent chalcedonies and colorful jaspers.

The extreme northwestern counties of Sioux and Dawes have many localities to find chalcedony, agates, jasper, fossil plants, and vertebrate remains. The breaks of the White River in Dawes County and the extensive rock beds east of Orella rank among the finest collecting grounds in the state. Nebraska is well known for its Nebraska Blue agate, a blue colored chalcedony that is the official state gemstone.

Agatized fossils and petrified wood can be found in the Sandhills country in Cherry County, extending along the Niobrara River eastward into Brown County. It can also be found in cuts and breaks in the hills along the Minnechaduza Creek, as well as all tributary canyons, creeks, and washes. The area around the confluence of the Loup River with the Platte River in Platte County is well known for its agates, chalcedony, jasper, moss opalite, and petrified wood. Other counties to find agate, jasper chalcedony, and petrified wood are Buffalo, Cass, Cheyenne, Deuel, Douglas, Garden, Keith, Jefferson, Morril, Nance, Nemaha, Otoe, Red Willow, Saunders, and Sheridan. In the eastern counties of the state, gravel quarries contain collectible amounts of chert, geodes, and fossils.

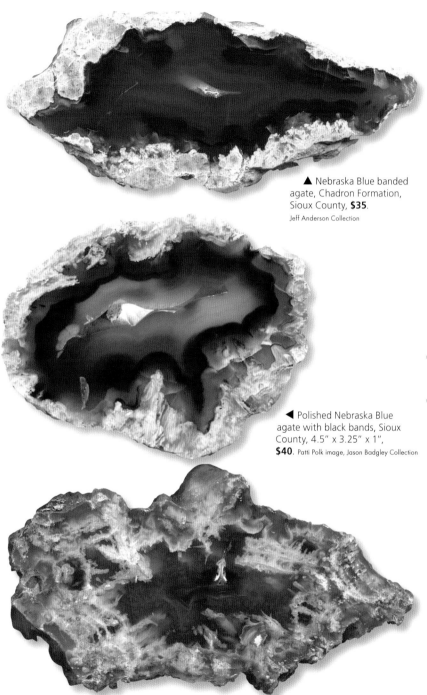

▲ Nebraska Blue banded agate, Chadron Formation, Sioux County, **$35**.
Jeff Anderson Collection

◀ Polished Nebraska Blue agate with black bands, Sioux County, 4.5" x 3.25" x 1", **$40**. Patti Polk image, Jason Badgley Collection

▲ Nebraska Blue agate with inclusions, Chadron Formation, Sioux County, **$40**. Jeff Anderson Collection

Nebraska

► Banded prairie agate. Crawford, Dawes County, 1.5" x 1.5" x 1", **$10 per pound**.
Patti Polk Collection

◄ Banded prairie agate, Crawford, Dawes County, 2.5" x 1.75" x 1", **$10 per pound**.
Patti Polk Collection

► Polished fortification Fairburn-type agate, Sioux County, 3" x 2.5" x 1.5", **$80**.
Patti Polk image, Jason Badgley Collection

Nebraska

◀ Water-worn banded Lake Superior agate from river gravels, Cass County, 2" x 1.75" x 1.75", **$15 per pound**. Patti Polk Collection

▶ Lacy, fortification prairie agate, Dawes County, 4.5" x 3.5" x 1", **$10 per pound**.
Patti Polk image, Jason Badgley Collection

◀ Rough lacy, banded "Bubblegum" agate, Dawes County, 1.5" x 1" x 1.5", **$10 per pound**.
Patti Polk Collection

Nebraska

Nevada

For more information, visit the Reno Gem and Mineral Society at www.renorockhounds.com and Southern Nevada Gem and Mineral Society at www.sngms.com.

Nevada lies within the Great Basin, and is made up of sedimentary rock broken and folded by granite intrusions and lavas from the Sierra Nevada uplift on the western edge of the state. The state overall is extremely dry and characterized by scores of short, high, rugged mountain chains that trend mainly from north to south, separated by arid valleys and plains. There are numerous locations for agate, jasper, chalcedony, chert, rhyolitic wonderstone, and petrified wood in the state of Nevada, and just a few of the counties include Churchill, Clark, Esmeralda, Humboldt, Lander, Lincoln, Lyon, Mineral, Nye, and Washoe. In the northwest section of the state, in Humboldt County, are located a number of fee-based mines that produce the beautiful precious opalized wood from the Virgin Valley region.

▲ Polished fire opal cabochon with matrix, Virgin Valley, Humboldt County, 1" x .5" x .25", **$40**. Patti Polk Collection

◀ Chalcedony-lined thunderegg, Jackpot, Elko County, **$25**.
Jeff Anderson Collection

▶ Polished moss agate nodule, Bull Canyon, Lyon County, 6" x 4" x 2", **$45**. Patti Polk image, Jason Badgley Collection

▲ Exterior of Mount Airy thunderegg. Patti Polk image, Jason Badgley Collection

◀ Blue chalcedony thunderegg, Mount Airy, Lander County, 3" x 3" x 2.5", **$40**.
Patti Polk image, Jason Badgley Collection

Nevada

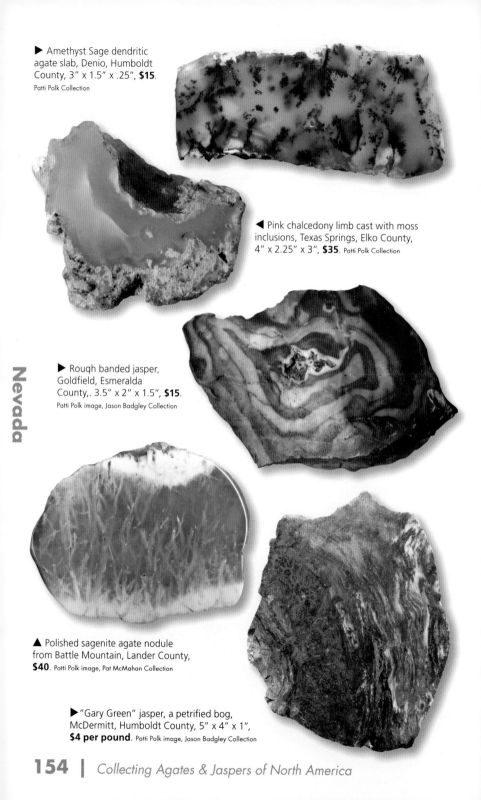

▶ Amethyst Sage dendritic agate slab, Denio, Humboldt County, 3" x 1.5" x .25", **$15**.
Patti Polk Collection

◀ Pink chalcedony limb cast with moss inclusions, Texas Springs, Elko County, 4" x 2.25" x 3", **$35**. Patti Polk Collection

▶ Rough banded jasper, Goldfield, Esmeralda County,. 3.5" x 2" x 1.5", **$15**.
Patti Polk image, Jason Badgley Collection

▲ Polished sagenite agate nodule from Battle Mountain, Lander County, **$40**. Patti Polk image, Pat McMahan Collection

▶ "Gary Green" jasper, a petrified bog, McDermitt, Humboldt County, 5" x 4" x 1", **$4 per pound**. Patti Polk image, Jason Badgley Collection

◀ "Lahontanite" brecciated jasp-agate slab, Fallon, Churchill County, 5" x 3" x .25", **$8**. Patti Polk Collection

▶ Banded thunderegg in rhyolite, Reno, Washoe County, **$30**. Jeff Anderson Collection

◀ Polished banded agate thunderegg, Black Rock Desert, Humboldt County, 3.5" x 3.25" x 1", **$35**. Patti Polk image, Jason Badgley Collection

Nevada

► Polished banded agate, Reno, Washoe County, **$40**.
Jeff Anderson Collection

▼ Petrified wood slab, Hubbard Basin, Elko County, 4" x 2.5" x .25", **$20**.
Patti Polk Collection

▲ Polished sagenite agate, McDermitt, Humboldt County, 4.5" x 2" x 1.5", **$45**. Patti Polk image, Jason Badgley Collection

Nevada

New Hampshire

Anyone with an interest in the hobby can contact Keene Mineral Club, www.keenemineralclub.50webs.com.

Known as the Granite State for its granite bedrock, the state was covered by Pleistocene glaciers that carved through the mountains and shaped the valleys that left many rivers and lakes behind. The White Mountains of the Appalachian chain stretch across the north while the level upland plateau in the south is noted for its isolated peaks. New Hampshire is primarily known for its minerals and gemstones, but jasper can be found in the Ammonoosuc River in Grafton County, at Jasper Mountain in Coos County, and in the counties of Belknap, Hanover (gravel pits), and Hillsborough (in gravels).

New Jersey

For more information about the hobby, visit
the North Jersey Mineralogical Society
at nojms.webs.com.

In this relatively small state sandwiched between the Hudson and the Delaware Rivers, the geology of New England merges with the geology of the Appalachian Highlands. The rock formations of this region are mainly folded and faulted limestones, sandstones, and shales, although three-fifths of New Jersey constitutes the Atlantic Coastal Plain, separated from the Highlands by the Triassic-aged Piedmont formation. Rivers, streams, and quarries in the northern and western half of the state contain much of the agate and jasper found here. Agate, chalcedony, jasper, and petrified wood can be found in Burlington, Camden, Hudson, Mercer (along the Delaware River), Morris, Passaic (also opal), Somerset, and Union counties. Tumbled chalcedony beach pebbles can be found at Cape May in Cape May County, and are locally referred to as "Cape May Diamonds," as well as small amounts of petrified wood. Unfortunately, most of the old agate locations are now paved over, but collecting can still often be done in gravel quarries with the owner's permission.

▲ Polished slab of rare Crocidolite in agate, Stirling, Morris County, **$150**. Barbara Grill image, Richard Hauck Collection

◀ Rough back side of Crocidolite in agate, Stirling, Morris County. Barbara Grill image, Richard Hauck Collection

◀ Cut front side of rare Crocidolite (blue asbestos) in agate, Stirling, Morris County, **$300**. Barbara Grill image, Richard Hauck Collection

▶ Rough agate with white quartz crystals, Paterson, Passaic County, **$50**. Barbara Grill image, Richard Hauck Collection

New Jersey

▲ Rough banded agate with black-tipped quartz crystals, Paterson, Passaic County, **$55**.
Barbara Grill image, Richard Hauck Collection

▶ Rough agate with black quartz crystals in vug, Paterson, Passaic County, **$50**.
Barbara Grill image, Richard Hauck Collection

▶ Botryoidal carnelian
with eyes, Stirling, Morris
County, **$60**. Barbara Grill
image, Richard Hauck Collection

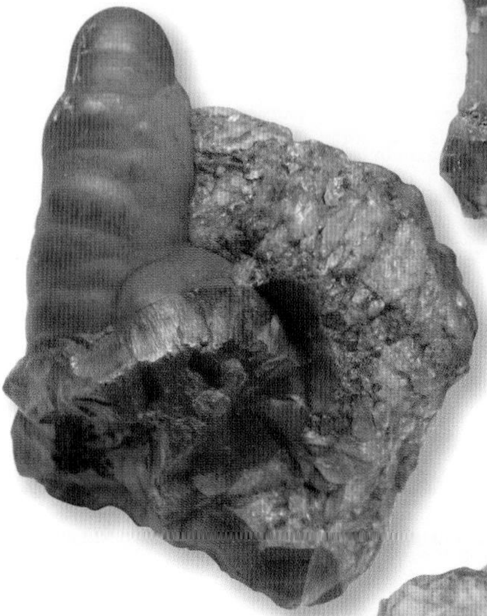

◀ Rough botryoidal carnelian,
Stirling, Morris County, **$50**.
Barbara Grill image, Richard Hauck Collection

▼ Botryoidal banded carnelian,
Stirling, Morris County, **$50**.
Barbara Grill image,
Richard Hauck Collection

◀ Botryoidal carnelian,
Stirling, Morris County,
$55. Barbara Grill image,
Richard Hauck Collection

◀ Polished lacy jasp-agate slab with druzy pocket, Paterson, Passaic County, **$50**. Barbara Grill image, Richard Hauck Collection

▶ Rough banded agate with parallax, Great Notch, Passaic County, **$55**.
Barbara Grill image, Richard Hauck Collection

◀ Orbicular jasp-agate, Paterson, Passaic County, **$50**.
Barbara Grill image, Richard Hauck Collection

▶ Polished fortification agate with quartz-filled pocket, Paterson, Passaic County, **$60**. Barbara Grill image, Richard Hauck Collection

New Jersey

New Mexico

For more information about collecting rocks and minerals, including a free download of a "Rockhounding Guide to New Mexico," visit The New Mexico Bureau of Geology & Mineral Resources at geoinfo.nmt.edu/faq/minerals.

New Mexico straddles the Continental Divide, and roughly bisected by the Rio Grande, exposes an array of Paleozoic rock formations in its semi-arid mountains and plateaus. Topographically, New Mexico is noted for its spacious grasslands, desert regions, broken mesas, volcanic zones, pine forests, and high mountain peaks. New Mexico is rich with many agate, jasper, chert, fossil, and petrified wood collecting locations. A very popular location for agate collecting is near the town of Deming in Luna County, where there are many opportunities to collect on both public and private properties, and to purchase fine examples of the local material at area rock shops. Beautifully banded and included geodes and thundereggs occur at the Baker Egg Mine, and good quality banded, sagenite, and plume agates can be collected nearby in the "Big Diggin's" vicinity.

Bernalillo, Catron, Dona Ana, Grant, Hidalgo, Lincoln, Luna, Rio Arriba, McKinley, Sandoval, San Juan, San Miguel, Santa Fe, Sierra, Socorro, Union, and Valencia are all counties where you can find varying amounts of collectible agates, jaspers, chalcedonies, fossils, and petrified and opalized woods.

◀ "Candy Rock," a rhyolitic wonderstone, Truth or Consequencs, Sierra County, 6" x 3" x .25", **$15**. Patti Polk image, Jason Badgley Collection

▶ "Eggzilla" thunderegg with sagenite, Deming, Luna County, 13" across the face, **$500**. Patti Polk image, Spanish Srirrup Rock Shop Collection

◀ Polished fortification slab with parallax and chromatography, Baker Egg Mine, Luna County, 3.5" x 2.25" x .25", **$80**. Patti Polk Collection

▶ Banded agate thunderegg, Hermanas, Luna County, **$65**. Jeff Anderson Collection

New Mexico

► Moss/plume agate, Lordsburg, Hidalgo County, **$30**.
Jeff Anderson Collection

◄ Polished sagenite agate, Silver City, Grant County, 3" x 2" x 1", **$35**.
Patti Polk image, Jason Badgley Collection

► Rough agate filled with dendrites, Red Hill, Catron County, 3.5" x 2.75" x 3", **$30**. Patti Polk Collection

◄ "Big Diggin's" polished agate with fortification and tubes, Deming, Luna County, 5" x 3.5" x 3", **$55**.
Patti Polk image, Jason Badgley Collection

◀ Colorful biconoid thunдеregg, Radium Springs, Dona Ana County, 6" across the face, **$200**.
Patti Polk image, Spanish Srirrup Rock Shop Collection

▼ Snowflake banded agate, Apache Creek, Catron County, 3.5" x 1.25" x 2", **$30**.
Patti Polk Collection

◀ Polished banded agate from Cook's Range, Luna County, **$25**.
Jeff Anderson Collection

▶ Thunderegg geode with pseudomorph stalks and quartz crystals, Baker Egg Mine, Luna County, 3" x 3" x 1.5", **$40**.
Patti Polk Collection

New Mexico

▲ Polished agate with snowflakes, moss and tubes, Apache Creek, Catron County, 7" x 2" x 1.5", **$60**.
Patti Polk Collection

▶ Typical banded "Big Diggin's" agate, Deming, Luna County, **$50**. Patti Polk image, Jason Badgley Collection

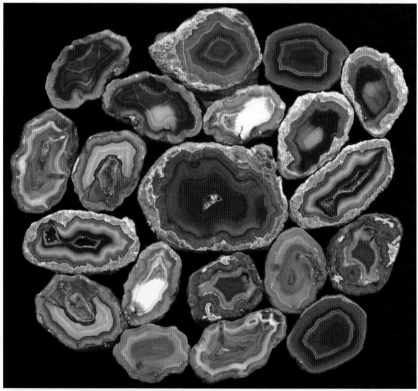

▲ Group of colorful agates from the Torpedo Beds, Hermanas, Luna County, **$20-$40 each**.
Jeff Anderson Collection

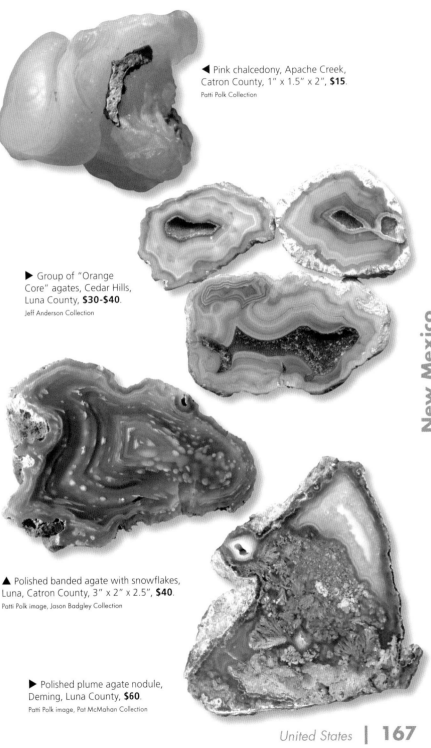

◀ Pink chalcedony, Apache Creek, Catron County, 1" x 1.5" x 2", **$15**.
Patti Polk Collection

▶ Group of "Orange Core" agates, Cedar Hills, Luna County, **$30-$40**.
Jeff Anderson Collection

▲ Polished banded agate with snowflakes, Luna, Catron County, 3" x 2" x 2.5", **$40**.
Patti Polk image, Jason Badgley Collection

▶ Polished plume agate nodule, Deming, Luna County, **$60**.
Patti Polk image, Pat McMahan Collection

New Mexico

▶ Polished thunderegg with sagenite, Baker Egg Mine, Luna County, 3.5" x 3" x 3", **$60**. Patti Polk image, Jason Badgley Collection

◀ Rough dendritic/plume agate, Reserve, Catron County, 2.5" x 2" x 1.5", **$25**. Patti Polk Collection

▲ "Apache Dendritic," a scenic rhyolite with dendritic patterns, Deming, Luna County. **$50**. Patti Polk image, Pat McMahan Collection

◀ "Lava Cap" thunderegg with fortification and sagenite, Deming, Luna County, 4" across the face, **$200**. Patti Polk image, Spanish Srirrup Rock Shop Collection

New York

For more information about gemstones and mineralogy, visit the New York Mineralogical Club at www.johnbetts-fineminerals.com/jhbnyc/nymc.htm.

In the western part of the state, New York has long rolling hills running toward lakes Ontario and Erie with many rivers and lakes formed by the action of ancient Pleistocene glaciers. The Alleghany Plateau in the south culminates at the Catskill Mountains, while Long Island is part of the coastal plain. The rugged Adirondacks in the northeast sweep down to plateaus of sedimentary rock although the mountains themselves are made of crystalline rocks similar to the Laurentians of Canada. Central New York is a plateau that becomes mountainous in the south and east where it meets the Appalachians. New York is most notable for its "Herkimer Diamonds," a water-clear, often doubly terminated quartz crystal found in Herkimer County. In the early settlements of the state, agates were once collected under what is now New York City. Today, there are a few locations in quarries, riverbanks, and gravels for agate, jasper, and bloodstone in Orange, Clinton, Monroe, and Suffolk (beach pebbles) counties. Agatized coral occurs in Livingston and Schoharie counties in river gravels and sedimentary exposures.

North Carolina

Founded in 1931, the Southern Appalachian Mineral Society is one of the oldest in the nation. For more information, visit www.main.nc.us/sams.

The sharply defined provinces of North Carolina constitute part of the Atlantic seaboard between the Atlantic Ocean and the Appalachian Mountains. From the tidewater swamps of the coast, the land rises in elevation along the western edge of the upper Coastal Plain before beginning the rolling hill country of the Piedmont formation. To the west, the land juts abruptly into the Blue Ridge, then dips sharply to the broad Carolina Highlands backed up against the Great Smoky Mountains. The Mountain and Piedmont regions expose folded, faulted, and broken rocks from Precambrian to Carboniferous ages, and the entire region is blanketed with metamorphic schists, gneisses, quartzites, and slates. North Carolina is best known for its minerals and pegmatite gemstones, but has a number of agate, jasper, and petrified wood occurrences, primarily in river and stream gravels. Counties that contain agate, carnelian, chalcedony, and jasper deposits include Anson, Buncombe, Cherokee, Clay (hyalite opal geodes), Cleveland, Cumberland, Grandville, Henderson, Mecklenburg, Michell, Moore, Polk (brecciated jasper), Stokes, and Wilkes. Petrified wood can be found in Quaternary river gravels in Anson (Pee Dee River), Cumberland, Durham, Halifax, Macom, Madison, Richmond, and Union counties.

▲ Banded chalcedony in silicified mircobreccia polished cabochon. Henderson County, 40mm long, **$45**. Mike Streeter Collection

▲ Group of rough silicified mircobreccia pieces, Henderson County, **$10 per pound**. Mike Streeter Collection

▲ Group of petrified wood pieces from Montgomery County, **$1 per pound**. Mike Streeter Collection

North Dakota

The North Dakota Geological Survey has information about local rocks and minerals. For more information, visit www.dmr.nd.gov/ndgs.

North Dakota consists of rock formations of greatly varied ages overlain by Quaternary soils and sediments. The eastern half, known as the Lowlands, once lay beneath the vanished waters of the great Pleistocene Lake Agassiz. West of the Red River Valley, escarpments rise to the glacial drift prairies of scattered lakes, moraines, and extensive, rolling, grass covered hills. Along the Little Missouri River lie the strongly eroded, famed Badlands, a region rich in fossils that date back to the era of the dinosaurs. From east to west and north to south, the alluvial gravels underlying the topsoil are rich in agate, chalcedony, jasper, and silicified wood. In the eastern counties occur Lake Superior-type agates, while the western counties yield Fairburn- and Montana-type moss agates. Adams, Billings, Burleigh, Grant, Hettinger, Kidder (fossils), McHenry, McKenzie, Morton, Pembina (fossils), Ramsey, Ransom, Stark, Ward, and Williams counties all have varying amounts of agate, jasper, and petrified wood.

◄ Montana-type agate from river gravels, McKenzie County, 3" x 1.5" 2", **$3 per pound**. Patti Polk Collection

► Moss agate from river gravels, Williams County, 2" x 1" x 2", **$5 per pound**. Patti Polk Collection

◄ Banded agate from river gravels, McKenzie County, 1.5" x 1.25" x 1", **$3 per pound**.
Patti Polk Collection

► Water polished petrified wood, Medora, Billings County, 4" x 3" x 1", **$5 per pound**.
Patti Polk Collection

North Dakota

Ohio

For more information about the hobby in Ohio, visit The Columbus Rock and Mineral Society, Inc., www.columbusrockandmineralsociety.org.

In Ohio, Paleozoic rock formations underlie the state's Pleistocene surface debris and Quaternary soils. Ages ago, Ohio lay beneath a shallow sea that received successive quantities of Ordovician, Silurian, Devonian, Mississippian and Pennsylvanian sediments. The state has been buried completely four times by glaciers, leaving the land surface nearly level but with some fairly

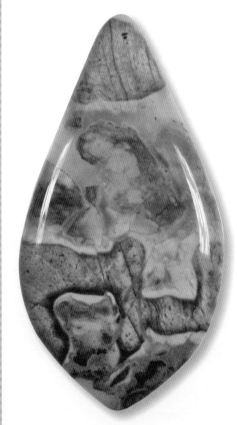

rugged low hills in the southeastern corner. There is little in Ohio in the way of agate and jasper locations, but agate, carnelian, chalcedony, chert, and jasper can be found in both Licking and Muskingum County, along with the well-known and colorful Vanport flint that occurs in the Flint Ridge area. Other flints can be found in the additional counties of Hocking, Perry, and Coshocton. Also, excavations in the underlying Upper Devonian (New Albany) shales occasionally produce pieces of silicified wood.

◀ Chert cabochon from Nethers Farm, Muskingum County, 57mm long, **$65**.
Mike Streeter Collection

► Nethers Farm chert, Muskingum County, **$6 per pound**.
Mike Streeter Collection

▲ Rough exterior of Ohio flint.
Patti Polk image, Jason Badgley Collection

► Cut face of rough Ohio flint, Muskingum County, 3″ x 2″ x 1.5″, **$4 per pound**.
Patti Polk image,
Jason Badgley Collection

Oklahoma

For more information about gems and minerals in Oklahoma, visit the Oklahoma Mineral and Gem Society at omgs-minerals.org.

Oklahoma occupies approximately 70,000 square miles in the southern part of the Great Plains region. The northwestern Oklahoma Panhandle is part of the arid, grassy Great Plains, while the Ozarks cross into the east central part of the prairie and die out on the Arbuckle Mountains plateau. From the Panhandle, the land slopes east and south to the southeastern corner of the state interrupted by a number of mountainous regions such as the Wichita and Ouachita ranges.

Southwestern Oklahoma, especially in Beckham and Tillman County, produce petrified wood and agates from regional gravel pits and stream beds. Along the Cimarron and North Canadian rivers, gravel bars contain agate, jasp-agate, jasper, chert, and petrified wood along with fossil bones and teeth of Pleistocene mammals. Canadian, Cimarron, Dewey, Greer, Harper, and Woods counties are all productive for agate and petrified wood collecting. Petrified wood also occurs in Potontoc, Murray, McCurtain, Kiowa, Cleveland, and Okfuskee counties.

▶ The reverse side of fossil algae from Black Mesa, Cimarron County. Patti Polk Collection

▼ Fossil algae from Black Mesa, Cimarron County, 3" x 1.5" x 1.5", **$20**.
Patti Polk Collection

▶ Rough exterior of juniper wood.
Patti Polk image, Jason Badgley Collection

◀ Polished face of petrified juniper wood, Grant County, 2" x 1.5" x 3", **$35**. Patti Polk image, Jason Badgley Collection

Oklahoma

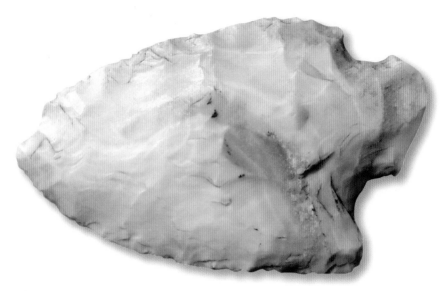

▲ Native American chert arrowhead, unknown location, 2.25" x 1.5" x .25", **$15**. Patti Polk Collection

▲ Chert from near
Spavinaw, Mayes County, **$5**.
Talequah Rock Club Collection

Oregon

For more information about agates and minerals, visit the Oregon Agate & Mineral Society, Inc., at www.oregonagate.org.

The geologic character of Oregon was formed during Tertiary times when millions of years of volcanic activity during the Oligocene and Miocene epochs raised the Cascade Mountains and layered nearly the whole surface of the state with thick beds of volcanic ash and flows of basalt. The Cascade Range divides the western portion of Oregon from the high, arid plateau county of the eastern two-thirds of the state. Northeastern Oregon is part of the basaltic Columbia Plateau, one of the largest raw lava regions of the world. Central and eastern Oregon are recognized as some of the best agate and jasper collecting locations in the United States, including many varieties of agates, jaspers, geodes, thundereggs, opal, fossils, and many types of agatized and opalized woods. The western region of the state also contains an abundant supply of agates and petrified wood in the creeks, rivers, and gravel bars, along with the coastal beaches. Many fine agates, jaspers, agatized wood, coral, bloodstone and fossils are found on Agate and Yachats beaches in Lincoln County, and other beaches along the Oregon shore including the beaches at Ten Mile, Heceta Head, and the beaches north and south of Yaquina Bay. The collecting areas are so numerous in Oregon that I will list only the most important locations here. Crook County: Carey Ranch, Ochoco and Maury Mountains, Paulina, Powell Butte, Prineville; Deschutes County: Hampton Butte; Harney County: Buchanan, Stinking Water; Jefferson County: Ashwood, Madras, Richardson Ranch; Lake County: Plush, Lakeview: Lane County: Trent; Linn County: Sweet Home, Holley, Thistle Creek; Malheur County: many locations including Brogan, Nyssa, Owyhee Dam, and Succor Creek; Morrow County: Heppner; Sherman County: Biggs and Wasco; Wasco County: Antelope.

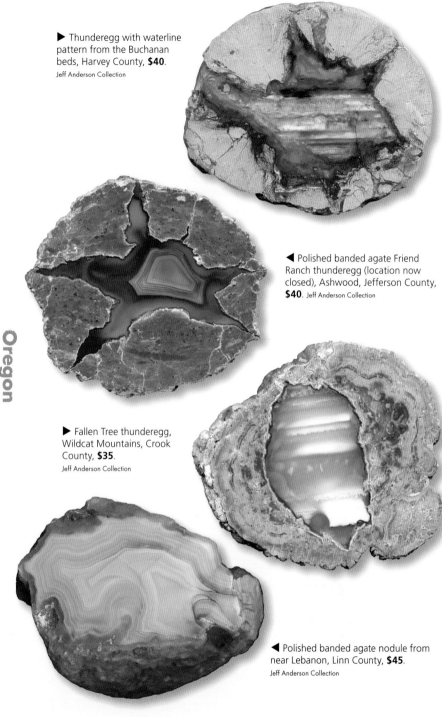

▶ Thunderegg with waterline pattern from the Buchanan beds, Harvey County, **$40**.
Jeff Anderson Collection

◀ Polished banded agate Friend Ranch thunderegg (location now closed), Ashwood, Jefferson County, **$40**. Jeff Anderson Collection

▶ Fallen Tree thunderegg, Wildcat Mountains, Crook County, **$35**.
Jeff Anderson Collection

◀ Polished banded agate nodule from near Lebanon, Linn County, **$45**.
Jeff Anderson Collection

Oregon

◀ Lucky Strike Mine moss thunderegg, Ochoco Mountains, Crook County, **$45**. Jeff Anderson Collection

▶ Agate slab with sagenite needles and small druzy pocket, Ochoco Mountains, Crook County, 2.25" x 1.75" x .25", **$15**. Patti Polk Collection

◀ Agate slab with sagenite and moss, Ochoco Mountains, Crook County, 3" x 2.75" x .25", **$18**. Patti Polk Collection

Oregon

◀ Exterior of biconoid showing bicone shape.
Patti Polk image, Jason Badgley Collection

▲ Biconoid thunderegg, Ochoco
Mountains, Crook County, 3.5" x 1.75" x 3.5",
$40. Patti Polk image, Jason Badgley Collection

▶ Exterior of water-worn moss
jasp-agate. Patti Polk image, Jason
Badgley Collection

◀ Water-worn
moss jasp-agate,
Agate Beach, Lincoln
County, 2.75" x 1.75" x .5",
$5. Patti Polk image, Jason Badgley Collection

Oregon

◀ Banded agate from Agate Beach, Lincoln County, 2.5" x 1" x 1.25", **$15**. Patti Polk image, Jason Badgley Collection

▶ Sagenite beach agate from Yachats, Lincoln County, 2.5" x 1.25" x .25", **$25**. Patti Polk image, Jason Badgley Collection

◀ Polished plume agate specimen from Carey Ranch, Prineville, Crook County, **$45**. Patti Polk image, Pat McMahan Collection

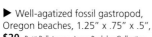

▶ Well-agatized fossil gastropod, Oregon beaches, 1.25" x .75" x .5", **$20**. Patti Polk image, Jason Badgley Collection

Oregon

▶ Polished white plume agate, Stinking Water, Harney County, **$40**.

Jeff Anderson Collection

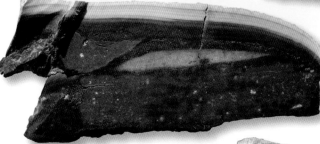

◀ "Bat Cave" picture jasper, Prineville, Crook County, 3.5" x 1.25" x .25", **$10**.

Patti Polk image, Jason Badgley Collection

Oregon

▶ Polished agate from Cape Meares, Tilamook County, 3" x 1.75" x 2.5", **$25**.

Patti Polk image, Jason Badgley Collection

▶ Polished Succor Creek thunderegg, Adrian, Malheur County, **$45**.

Jeff Anderson Collection

▶ Rough carnelian banded agate, Sweet Home, Linn County, 3" x 1.5" x 2", **$14 per pound**.
Patti Polk Collection

◀ "Chicken Track" picture jasper, with aptly named chicken track surface formations, Malheur County, 3.5" x 1.5" x 3", **$4 per pound**. Patti Polk image, Jason Badgley Collection

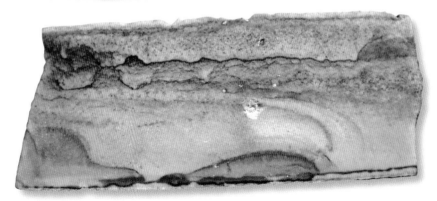

▲ "Chicken Track" picture jasper, **$4 per pound**. Patti Polk image, Jason Badgley Collection

►Polished plume agate slab from Carey Ranch, Prineville, Crook County, 4" x 3.5" x .25", **$45**. Patti Polk image, Jason Badgley Collection

▼ Polished Eagle Rock moss agate, Prineville, Crook County, 4.5" x 2" x 1", **$45**. Patti Polk image, Jason Badgley Collection

Oregon

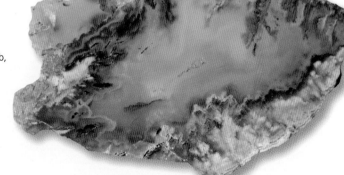

► Plume agate slab, Graveyard Point, Malheur County, 3" x 1.75" x .25", **$10 per pound**. Patti Polk Collection

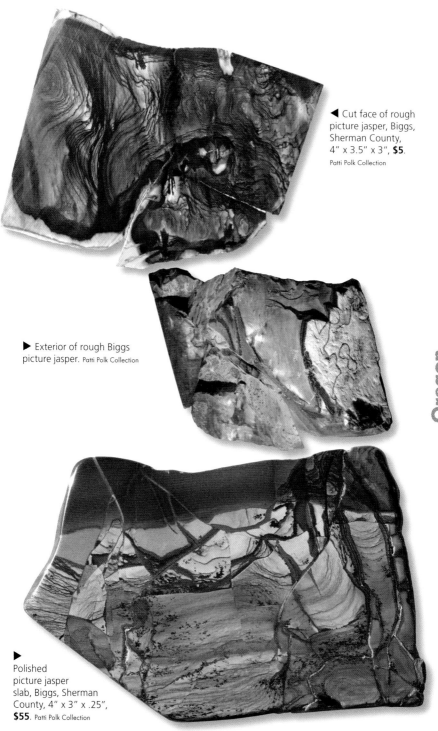

◀ Cut face of rough picture jasper, Biggs, Sherman County, 4" x 3.5" x 3", **$5**.
Patti Polk Collection

▶ Exterior of rough Biggs picture jasper. Patti Polk Collection

▶
Polished picture jasper slab, Biggs, Sherman County, 4" x 3" x .25", **$55**. Patti Polk Collection

Oregon

► Crooked Creek pink chalcedony limb cast, Paulina, Crook County, 1.5" x 1.25" x 4", **$10 per pound**. Patti Polk Collection

► Holley Blue agate pseudomorph over dogtooth calcite, Sweet Home, Linn County, 10" high, **$300**. Chuck Bennett Collection

Oregon

◄ Rough Holley Blue agate, Sweet Home, Linn County, 1.25" x 1" x 1.5", **$35 per pound**. Patti Polk Collection

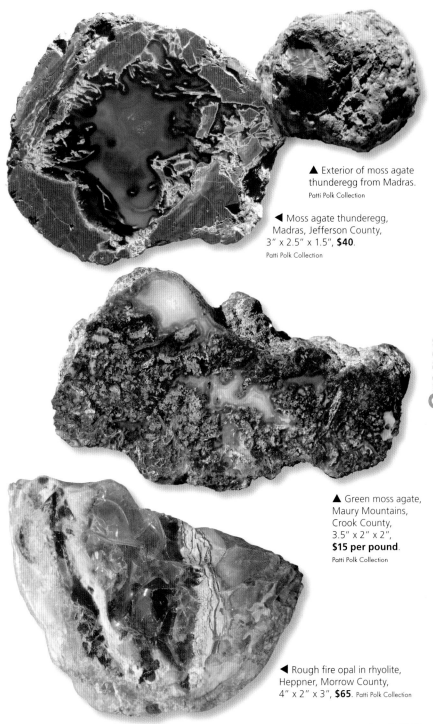

▲ Exterior of moss agate thunderegg from Madras.
Patti Polk Collection

◀ Moss agate thunderegg, Madras, Jefferson County, 3" x 2.5" x 1.5", **$40**.
Patti Polk Collection

▲ Green moss agate, Maury Mountains, Crook County, 3.5" x 2" x 2", **$15 per pound**.
Patti Polk Collection

◀ Rough fire opal in rhyolite, Heppner, Morrow County, 4" x 2" x 3", **$65**. Patti Polk Collection

Oregon

► Priday Bed moss thunderegg slab from Richardson Ranch, Madras, Jefferson County, 4" x 3.5" .25", **$45**. Patti Polk image, Jason Badgley Collection

◄ Polished Priday Bed plume agate thunderegg from Richardson Ranch, Madras, Jefferson County, **$90**.
Patti Polk image, Pat McMahan Collection

► Polished Richardson Ranch tube agate cabochon by the author, Madras, Jefferson County, 40mm x 30mm, **$55**. Patti Polk Collection

◄ Thunderegg with pink moss inclusions from Richardson Ranch, Madras, Jefferson County, 3" x 2" x 2", **$35**. Patti Polk Collection

Oregon

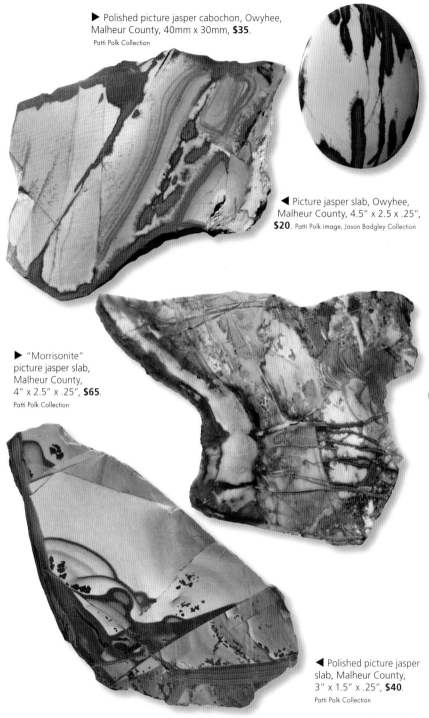

▶ Polished picture jasper cabochon, Owyhee, Malheur County, 40mm x 30mm, **$35**.
Patti Polk Collection

◀ Picture jasper slab, Owyhee, Malheur County, 4.5" x 2.5 x .25", **$20**. Patti Polk image, Jason Badgley Collection

▶ "Morrisonite" picture jasper slab, Malheur County, 4" x 2.5" x .25", **$65**.
Patti Polk Collection

◀ Polished picture jasper slab, Malheur County, 3" x 1.5" x .25", **$40**.
Patti Polk Collection

Oregon

▶ Blue Mountain polished picture jasper nodule, Malheur County, 3.5" x 3" x 2.25", **$40**.
Patti Polk image, Jason Badgley Collection

◀ Polished petrified wood, Malheur County, 3" x 1.5" x 2", **$25**.
Patti Polk Collection

Oregon

▶ "Polka Dot" agate slab, Madras, Jefferson County, 3" x 1.5" x .25", **$18**. Patti Polk image, Jason Badgley Collection

◀ Polished plume agate slab, Powell Butte, Crook County, 3" x 2.75" x .25", **$35**. Patti Polk image, Jason Badgley Collection

◀ Banded agate slab with rare stibnite and realgar inclusions, Trent, Lane County, 2.5" x 1.5" x 2", **$55**. Patti Polk image, Jason Badgley Collection

▶ Rough green "Spiderweb" jasper with rhyolite, Malheur County, 4.5" x 4" x 4", **$6 per pound**. Patti Polk Collection

◀ Polished sagenite in agate specimen from Thistle Creek, Linn County, **$60**. Chuck Bennett Collection

▶ Red and black webbed "Spiderman" jasper slab, Malheur County, 4" x 3.5" x .25", **$6 per pound**. Patti Polk Collection

Oregon

Pennsylvania

For more information about rocks and
minerals in Pennsylvania, visit the
Central Pennsylvania Rock and Mineral
Club, Inc., at www.rockandmineral.org.

The basic underlying formation in Pennsylvania consists
of coarse Pottsville conglomerate sediments eroded from the
western slopes of Appalachia, and characterized by rolling hills
and ridges cut by narrow valleys. Eastern Pennsylvania falls
within the coastal plain composed of marine deposits, while
the highlands are constructed of crystalline and volcanic rocks
culminating in the Allegheny plateau. Although Pennsylvania is
most known for its great coal deposits, there are locations where
agate, jasper, chert, and petrified wood occur in fields, quarries,
and stream gravels. Counties include Adams, Armstrong (petrified
wood in streambeds), Bedford, Bucks, Carbon, Centre (oolitic
chert) Cumberland, Dauphin, Franklin (red jasper near Caledonia
State Park), Lancaster (bloodstone, banded chalcedony, common
opal, prase), Lehigh, Monroe (agatized coral), Montgomery,
Northampton (oolitic flint and fossils from limestone quarries),
Westmoreland, and York (petrified wood).

Rhode Island

For more information about rock and mineral hunting, visit the Rhode Island Mineral Hunters at rimh.us.

Rhode Island, the smallest and most densely populated of the 50 states, has a western boundary only 42 miles long and a maximum width across the south of 35 miles. The land surface is rolling and hilly cut with short, swift streams draining into ocean bays, and having been scoured to bedrock by Ice Age glaciers, sedimentary deposits, other than Pleistocene to Recent, are quite rare. Agate collecting locations are limited, but agate, chalcedony, and jasper have occurred in pockets at the Cumberland and Diamond Hill quarries in Providence County, jasper pebbles have been reported in gravel deposits near Bristol in Bristol County, and pebbles of carnelian have been found on the shores of Narragansett Bay in Washington County.

South Carolina

For more information about gems and minerals, visit the Lowcountry Gem and Mineral Society at www.lowcountrygemandmineralsociety.org.

South Carolina divides roughly into three main geological regions: the Coastal Plain, separated from the Piedmont plateau by the Fall Line, and the small Inner Piedmont in the extreme northwestern corner as part of the Blue Ridge Mountains. The underlying rock formations of the Inner Piedmont are primarily schists and granites of Precambrian to early Paleozoic age, cut by granite intrusives. In the northwest, the regional metamorphism that accompanied intense folding and faulting has produced widespread conglomerates, marble, quartzites, and schists, and the accompanying fine gemstones that the state is known for. Chert has been found in Allendale County, blue jasper in Abbeville County, Savannah River agates in Aiken County, petrified wood in Darlington, Florence, Fairfield, and Marlboro counties; agate, chalcedony and fossil shark teeth in beach gravels around Myrtle Beach in Horry County; and banded chalcedony in silicified microbreccia in Greenville County.

▲ Silicified microbreccia polished cabochon, Greenville County, 41mm long, **$10**.
Mike Streeter Collection

▲ Silicified microbreccia polished cabochon, Greenville County, 52mm long, **$65**. Mike Streeter Collection

▲ Rough silicified microbreccia from Greenville County, **$2 per pound**. Mike Streeter Collection

▲ Banded chalcedony in silicified microbreccia polished cabochon, Greenville County, 54mm long, **$35**. Mike Streeter Collection

▲ Banded chalcedony in silicified microbreccia polished cabochon, Greenville County, 47mm long, **$65**. Mike Streeter Collection

▲ Banded chalcedony in silicified microbreccia, Greenville County, **$8 per pound**. Mike Streeter Collection

▲ Banded chalcedony in silicified microbreccia, Greenville County, **$8 per pound**. Mike Streeter Collection

South Dakota

For more information about gems and minerals, visit the Sioux Empire Gem and Mineral Society at www.segams.org.

South Dakota is a fairly level, glaciated plain to the east of the Missouri River. Beneath most of the glacial drift east of the Missouri River are Cretaceous-Age shales, sandstones, and limestone. To the west lie open, arid prairies, and in the southwest corner of the state lie the granitic Black Hills atop the famed Dakota Sandstone, which underlies most of the Great Plains region. In the extreme south central area of the state are pine-covered buttes, rolling sand dunes, and the badlands topography that South Dakota is famous for. The eastern counties of the state yield agate, chalcedony, and jasper in the river gravels and very fine agates can be found on the badlands in the southwest area of the state. Here you will find the beautiful fortification agates known as "Fairburns," so named due to their proximity to the town of Fairburn in Custer County. Not far from there is another location for similar agates, from the area of Teepee Canyon, also in Custer County. There are many locations throughout the state for agate collecting that can be found using field collecting guidebooks. Agate collecting areas include the counties of Fall River, Custer, Harding, Jackson, Jones, Meade, Minnehaha, and Pennington. Petrified wood, including petrified cycad, occurs in Campbell, Corson, Fall River, Lawrence, and Todd counties.

▶ Rough Fairburn fortification agate, Black Hills, Custer County, **$150**.
Jeff Anderson Collection

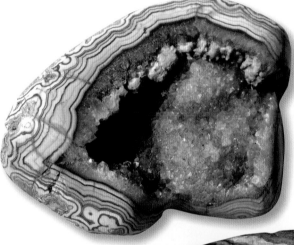

◀ Rough Fairburn agate with druzy quartz crystals, Custer County. 2.5" x 1.75" x 1", **$50**.
Patti Polk Collection

▶ Colorful fortification Fairburn agate, Custer County, **$300**.
Tom Shearer Collection

◀ Small polished Teepee Canyon fortification agate, Custer County, 2″ x 1.5″ x 1″, **$40**. Patti Polk Collection

▶ Rough Teepee Canyon agate with quartz crystals in center, Custer County, 2.5″ x 2″ x 2″, **$10 per pound**. Patti Polk Collection

◀ Beautiful Fairburn agate, Custer County, 2″ x 1.5″ x 1″, **$80**. Patti Polk Collection

▲ Smooth exterior of the sedimentary nodule.
Patti Polk Collection

▶ Fortification agate formed in a sedimentary nodule, Teepee Canyon, Custer County, 3.25" x 3" x 3", **$10 per pound**.
Patti Polk Collection

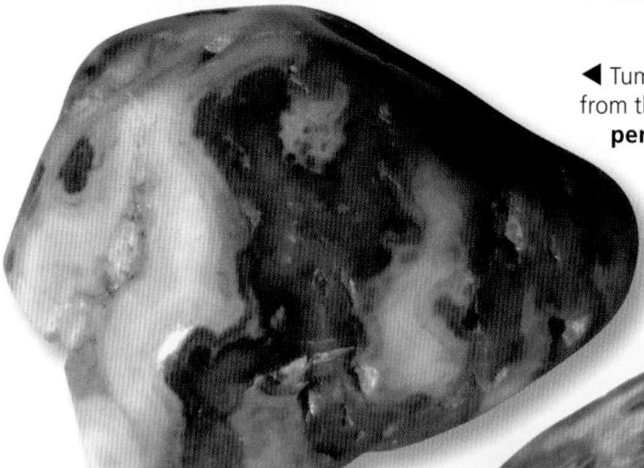

◀ Tumble polished "Bubblegum" agate from the badlands, 1" x 1" x 1.75", **$10 per pound**. Patti Polk Collection

▶ Colorful prairie agate from the badlands, 1.75" x 1.52" x 1.5", **$10 per pound**. Patti Polk Collection

Tennessee

For more information about gems and minerals, visit the Mid-Tennessee Gem and Mineral Society at www.mtgms.org.

Tennessee is separated into three main geologic landforms: river valley plain, highlands and basins, and mountains. In the east are the Great Smoky Mountains and the Cumberland Plateau; the central region is gentle rolling grassland, and the western part of the state is alluvial river bottomlands. Bordered by the Mississippi River to the west, Tennessee is primarily sedimentary rock, except for the Appalachian Mountains in the eastern part of the state. Tennessee is known mainly for its colorful Paint Rock agate and Horse Mountain agate which, when cut properly, may display the rainbow iris effect. Counties where various agates, cherts, and jaspers occur are Bedford (also agatized corals), Coffee, Lawrence, Putnam, Rutherford, Shelby (agatized fossils in gravels), Washington, Wayne (chert, flint, agatized fossils), and White. Paint Rock agate has been found in Franklin and Grundy counties.

◀ Polished Tennessee Puddingstone, **$8 per pound**. Mike Streeter Collection

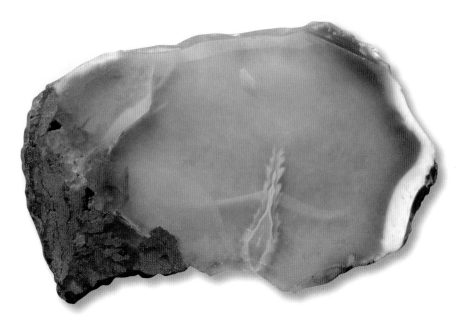

▲ Iris agate slab in normal light, Horse Mountain, Bedford County, 3.5" x 2" x .12". Patti Polk image, Jason Badgley Collection

▲ Iris agate slab showing iris effect in the proper light, **$75**. Patti Polk image, Jason Badgley Collection

◄ Polished jasper cabochon, Bumpass Cove, Washington County, 38mm long, **$20**. Mike Streeter Collection

▲ Rough jasper, Bumpass Cove, Washington County, **$6 per pound**. Mike Streeter Collection

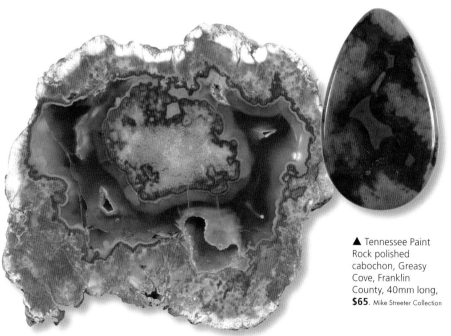

▲ Tennessee Paint Rock polished cabochon, Greasy Cove, Franklin County, 40mm long, **$65**. Mike Streeter Collection

▲ Tennessee Paint Rock nodule, Greenhaw, Franklin County, **$65**. Jeff Anderson Collection

Texas

For a listing of rock, gem and mineral clubs in Texas, visit www.the-vug.com/vug/vugclubs.html#texas.

Texas contains a great variety of geologic regions. The state is bisected by a series of faults that trend southwest to northeast across the state. Southeastern Texas is made up of sandy coastal plain sediments, while rolling prairies extend across central and north Texas. In the northwest lies the Texas Panhandle, an arid Great Plains region, and below to the west, are rugged mountain ranges crested by El Capitan, the highest point in the state. The main collecting areas in Texas can basically be grouped into three regions the gravel beds of the Rio Grande delta area, the Big Bend area, and the broad area known as the Catahoula formation, which extends from the lower Rio Grande to the Louisiana border. The Catahoula formation is known for petrified fern, silicified palm wood, and opalized Golden Pine wood. Many fine collectible agates come from Texas and include the beautiful plume agates from the famous Woodward and Walker ranches, as well as the striking bouquet agates from the Needle Peak area near Marfa. Collectible agate, jasper, and chert, can be found in Brewster, Jeff Davis, Kinney, Maverick, Presidio, Reeves, and Zapata counties. Petrified wood and palm can be found in Bastrop, Burleson, Colorado, Duval, Fayette, Grimes, Karnes, Live Oak, McMullen, Potter, Sabine, Starr, Trinity, Val Verde, and Zapata counties.

▲ Plume agate from Bishop Ranch, Alpine, Brewster County, **$40**. Jeff Anderson Collection

▲ Polished plume agate, Balmorhea,
Reeves County, **$50**. Jeff Anderson Collection

▶ Banded agate with moss inclusions,
Balmorhea, Reeves County, **$40**.
Jeff Anderson Collection

◀ Polished multi-color
plume agate nodule,
Marfa, Presido County,
$65. Jeff Anderson Collection

▶ Plume agate slab,
Marfa, Presido County,
2.75″ x 1.75″ x .25″,
$30. Patti Polk Collection

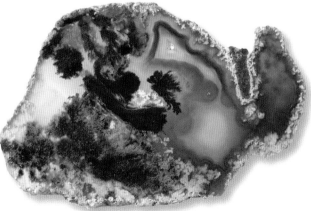

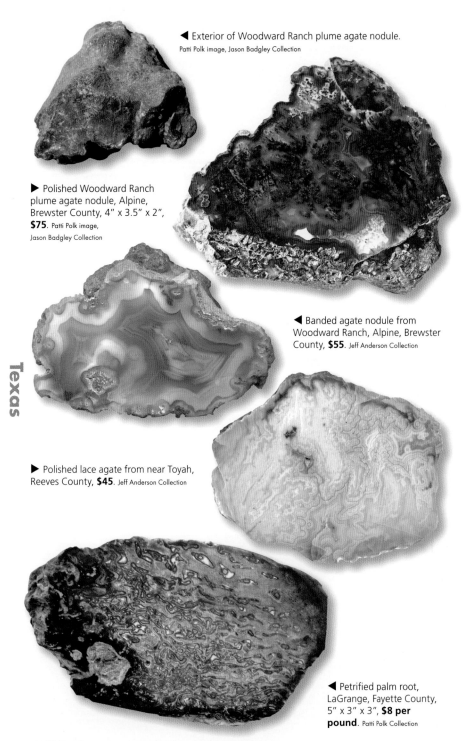

◀ Exterior of Woodward Ranch plume agate nodule.
Patti Polk image, Jason Badgley Collection

▶ Polished Woodward Ranch plume agate nodule, Alpine, Brewster County, 4" x 3.5" x 2", **$75**. Patti Polk image, Jason Badgley Collection

◀ Banded agate nodule from Woodward Ranch, Alpine, Brewster County, **$55**. Jeff Anderson Collection

▶ Polished lace agate from near Toyah, Reeves County, **$45**. Jeff Anderson Collection

◀ Petrified palm root, LaGrange, Fayette County, 5" x 3" x 3", **$8 per pound**. Patti Polk Collection

Texas

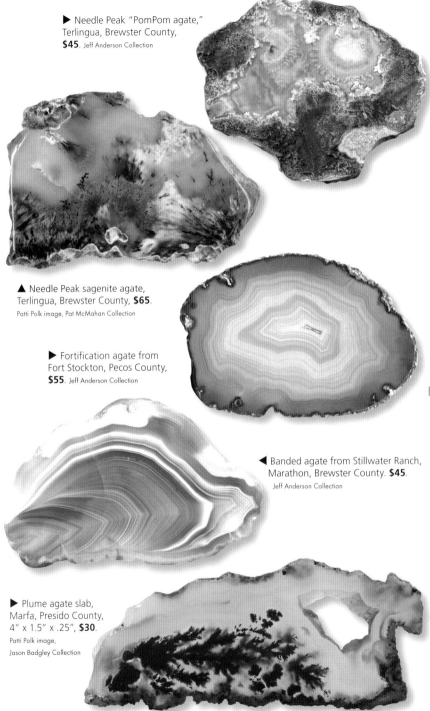

▶ Needle Peak "PomPom agate," Terlingua, Brewster County, **$45**. Jeff Anderson Collection

▲ Needle Peak sagenite agate, Terlingua, Brewster County, **$65**.
Patti Polk image, Pat McMahan Collection

▶ Fortification agate from Fort Stockton, Pecos County, **$55**. Jeff Anderson Collection

◀ Banded agate from Stillwater Ranch, Marathon, Brewster County. **$45**.
Jeff Anderson Collection

▶ Plume agate slab, Marfa, Presido County, 4" x 1.5" x .25", **$30**.
Patti Polk image,
Jason Badgley Collection

Texas

▶ Banded agate nodule, Van Horn Mountains, Culberson County, **$40**. Jeff Anderson Collection

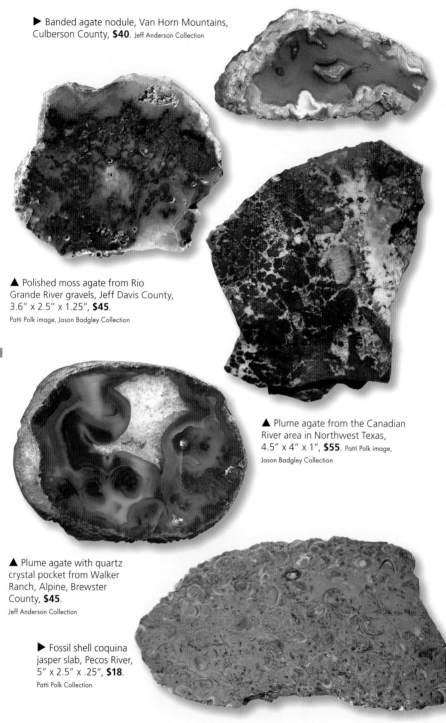

▲ Polished moss agate from Rio Grande River gravels, Jeff Davis County, 3.6" x 2.5" x 1.25", **$45**.
Patti Polk image, Jason Badgley Collection

▲ Plume agate from the Canadian River area in Northwest Texas, 4.5" x 4" x 1", **$55**. Patti Polk image, Jason Badgley Collection

▲ Plume agate with quartz crystal pocket from Walker Ranch, Alpine, Brewster County, **$45**.
Jeff Anderson Collection

▶ Fossil shell coquina jasper slab, Pecos River, 5" x 2.5" x .25", **$18**.
Patti Polk Collection

Texas

Utah

For more information about rocks and minerals, visit the Mineral Collectors of Utah at sites.google.com/site/mincollutah.

The topography of Utah is dramatically halved between the low-lying desert of the Great Basin region in the west and an extremely rugged mountain and plateau in the eastern half, bound on the north by the Uinta Mountains, which follow Wyoming's southern border. The Wasatch Range bisects the state from the Idaho boundary to the south, making an abrupt transition between the mountain and plateau region to the east and the arid desert playas and saline lakes of the western half. The southeastern one-third of Utah comprises the major portions of the sandstone plateau and canyon region. Here agate occurs in many varieties, and there is an abundance of jasper, colorful petrified wood, and agatized fossils to be found in numerous locations within the Morrison formation exposures. Many agates and jaspers are also found to the west of

the Cascades in the lower desert regions. Just some of the counties statewide where agate, jasper, and petrified wood can be found are Beaver, Emery, Garfield, Grand, Iron, Kane, Juab (geodes), San Juan, Washington, and Wayne.

▲ Banded agate with quartz center geode, Dugway, Juab County, 3" x 2.5" x 2.5", **$30**. Patti Polk image, Jason Badgley Collection

▲ Well-formed, large agate after barite nodule, Yellow Cat, Grand County, 6" x 5" x 2", **$60**.
Patti Polk Collection

▲ Small agate after barite nodule with polished end, Yellow Cat, Grand County, 3" x 1.5" x 3", **$40**. Patti Polk Collection

▲ Back side of dinosaur bone.
Patti Polk image, Doris Banks Collection

◀ Rough dinosaur bone, Moab, Grand County, 6" x 6" x 4", **$150**.
Patti Polk image, Doris Banks Collection

▲ Exterior of coprolite nodule.
Patti Polk image, Jason Badgley Collection

▶ Polished coprolite (dino dung) nodule, Henry Mountains, Garfield County, 2.25" x 2.25" x 1", **$30**.
Patti Polk image, Jason Badgley Collection

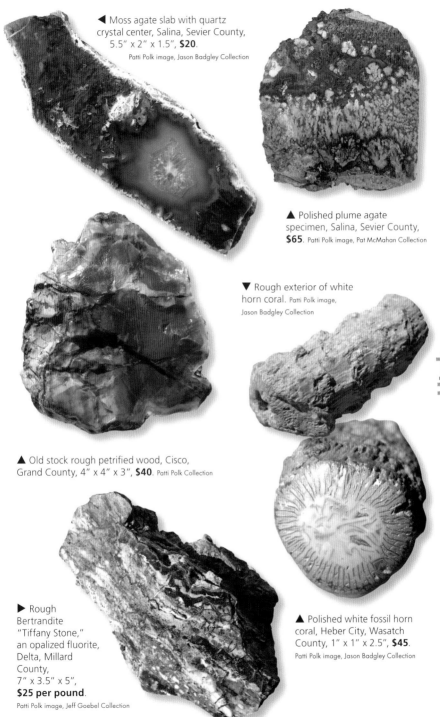

◄ Moss agate slab with quartz crystal center, Salina, Sevier County, 5.5" x 2" x 1.5", **$20**.
Patti Polk image, Jason Badgley Collection

▲ Polished plume agate specimen, Salina, Sevier County, **$65**. Patti Polk image, Pat McMahan Collection

▼ Rough exterior of white horn coral. Patti Polk image, Jason Badgley Collection

▲ Old stock rough petrified wood, Cisco, Grand County, 4" x 4" x 3", **$40**. Patti Polk Collection

▶ Rough Bertrandite "Tiffany Stone," an opalized fluorite, Delta, Millard County, 7" x 3.5" x 5", **$25 per pound**.
Patti Polk image, Jeff Goebel Collection

▲ Polished white fossil horn coral, Heber City, Wasatch County, 1" x 1" x 2.5", **$45**.
Patti Polk image, Jason Badgley Collection

Utah

▲ Polished banded black agate, Levan, Juab County, 3" x 1.5" x 2", **$25**. Patti Polk image, Jason Badgley Collection

▲ Polished agate with waterline banding, Levan, Juab County, 4" x 2.5" x .75", **$25**. Patti Polk image, Jason Badgley Collection

▲ Brilliantly colored rough petrified wood, Hansen Creek, Garfield County, 3" x 2.5" x 2", **$65**. Patti Polk image, Doris Banks Collection

▲ Very well-silicified polished flowering tube cave onyx, Levan, Juab County, 3.5" x 2.75" x 1", **$45**. Patti Polk Collection

◄ Old stock colorful petrified wood, Yellow Cat, Grand County, 3.5" x 3" x 4", **$50**. Patti Polk Collection

▲ Polished petrified wood specimen, Henry Mountains, Garfield County, 4.5" x 2.25" x 2", **$45**. Patti Polk image, Jason Badgley Collection

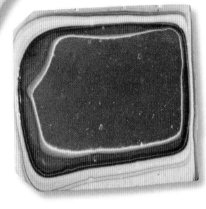

▲ Polished red fossil horn coral, Riley Canyon, Juab County, 1.25" x 1" x 2.5", **$35**.
Patti Polk image, Jason Badgley Collection

▲ Scenic rhyolitic wonderstone slab, Salina, Sevier County, 1.5" x 1.25" x .25", **$3 per pound**. Patti Polk image, Jason Badgley Collection

▲ Rough hyalite "Bubble Opal" with cut face, Milford, Beaver County, 4.5" x 1" x 2", **$45**. Patti Polk Collection

▶ Banded wonderstone slab, Vernon Hills, Tooele County, 3.5" x 2" x .25", **$3 per pound**. Patti Polk image, Jason Badgley Collection

◀ Petrified wood limb, Escalante, Garfield County, 1.5" x 1" x 3", **$4 per pound**. Patti Polk Collection

Utah

▲ "Pigeon Blood" agate slab, Moab, Grand County, 4" x 3" x .25", **$4 per pound**. Patti Polk Collection

◀ Moss agate slab, Brian Head, Iron County, 3.5" x 2.25" x .25", **$10**. Patti Polk Collection

Vermont

For more information about
gems and minerals, visit the Burlington
Gem and Mineral Club at
www.burlingtongemandmineralclub.org.

Although beautiful, Vermont has little to offer the agate and jasper collector, since the basal formation of Vermont is granitic and not of the volcanic type to create the environment necessary to produce the desired chalcedonies, agates, and jaspers. East of the Green Mountain system lie the Granite Hills, well named because of the excellent monument granite and building stone quarried in many places. The granite industry is centered at Barre in Washington County, while Rutland at the south end of the Green Mountains in Rutland County is famed for its production of fine marble. There is little in the way of agate locations in Vermont, except for reports of red jasper, chert, jasp-agate, and agate from the old Parrott quarry in Chittenden County and a small amount of agate exposed in a road cut near Adams Brook in Windham County. Fossil gastropods may periodically occur in limestone quarries in Grand Isle County.

Virginia

More information about rockhounding in Virginia, including a list of gem and mineral clubs, can be found at the Virginia Rockhounders site at varockhound.com/rockhound-info.

Virginia divides into the regions of the Tidewater or Eastern Section and the Piedmont Plateau, reaching west to the Blue Ridge Mountains. The granitoid nature of Virginia's Precambrian and Cambrian structures has produced many pegmatite formations, and numerous gem and mineral species appear in the exposures and erosional debris. Although Virginia is predominately pegamatite bearing, there are a few locations where agate, chalcedony, chert, and jasper can be found, including Albemarle, Arlington, Agusta, Bland, and Fairfax counties, mainly in quarries and gravels. Petrified wood can be found in Chesterfield, Powhatan, Prince William, and Stafford counties in fields, quarries and gravels.

Washington

For more information about agates and jaspers in Washington, visit the Washington Agate and Mineral Society at wamsolympia.wordpress.com.

The state of Washington has a varied and complex topography. The Cascade Mountains divide the state into a forested, wet western section and an eastern two-thirds that is arid, basaltic, and cut by the great gorges of the Columbia River and its tributaries. Puget Sound bisects the northern half of the western portion with its salt waters to create the Olympic Peninsula to the west. Throughout the western area of the state, there are locations containing agatized clams and oysters, along with other types of Miocene fossils. During the 30 million years of the Oligocene, Miocene and Pliocene epochs when the Cascades were rising, fluid lavas poured from the volcanoes to fill the existing valleys, lakes and swamps. The lavas covered much of the western parts of the state and almost all of eastern Washington, and overlapped into Canada, Idaho, and Oregon. The flows of basalt erupted again and again, and over time the forests were buried under thick blankets of volcanic ash, rich in silica, creating fine petrified woods. As the volcanoes poured out their lavas, the Columbia River maintained its original westward course and its gravel bars still contain large quantities of agates, jaspers, and petrified woods today. Collecting locations productive with agate, carnelian, chalcedony, jasper, and petrified wood include Benton, Clallam, Cowlitz, Douglas, Franklin, Grant, Grays Harbor (beaches and stream beds), Kittitas (Ellensburg), King, Klickitat, Jefferson (beaches), Lewis, Lincoln, Skagit (beaches), Thurston, and Yakima counties.

▲ Colorful polished agate from Chandler Butte, Benton County, **$60**. Patti Polk image, Pat McMahan Collection

▲ Exterior of Kalama banded agate, Cowlitz County. **$20**. Patti Polk image, Jason Badgley Collection

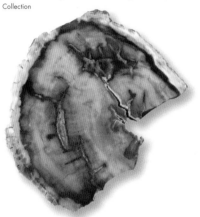

▲ Partial round of petrified wood with fortification agate zones, Saddle Mountains, Grant County, 4.5" x 4" x 1", **$40**. Patti Polk Collection

▲ Polished "Ellensburg Blue" agate with waterline and moss inclusions, Ellensburg, Kittitas County, **$55** Patti Polk image, Pat McMahan Collection

▼ Slab of petrified wood, Saddle Mountains, Grant County, 4" x 2" x .25", **$40**. Patti Polk Collection

▲ Banded agate from river gravels, Pasco, Franklin County, 1.5" x 2" x 1.25", **$20**. Mark Berreth image, Von Anderson- Berreth Collection

▲ Agatized fossil clamshell, 1" x 1" x .5",
$25. Patti Polk image, Jason Badgley Collection

▲ Carnelian with banding, Richland, Benton
County, 2.5" x 1.25" x 2.25", **$18**.
Mark Berreth Collection

◀ Exterior of Lucas Creek banded agate.
Patti Polk image, Jason Badgley Collection

▶ Banded agate from Lucas
Creek, Lewis County,
3.5" x 1.5" x 1.5", **$25**.
Patti Polk image,
Jason Badgley Collection

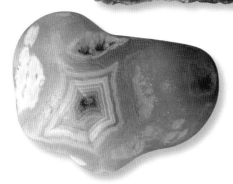

▲ Banded agate from river gravels, Pasco,
Franklin County, 3.25" x 1.75" x 1.75", **$20**.
Mark Berreth Collection

▶ Little Naches River thunderegg, Yakima,
Yakima County, **$35**. Jeff Anderson Collection

Washington

◀ Polished banded agate nodule, Kalama, Cowlitz County, 3" x 2.5" x 1", **$25**.
Patti Polk image, Jason Badgley Collection

▶ Polished jasp-agate, Tahoma Peak, Pierce County, 3.5" x 1.5" x 1.5", **$40**. Patti Polk image, Jason Badgley Collection

◀ Carnelian with sagenite inclusions, Green River, King County, **$50**. Chuck Bennett Collection

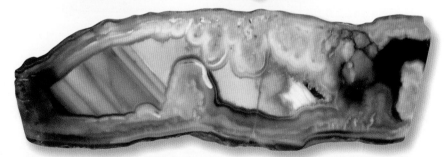

▲ Polished jasp-agate specimen from Mount Rainier, Pierce County, **$45**. Patti Polk image, Pat McMahan Collection

Washington

West Virginia

For more information about the hobby,
visit the West Virginia Fossil Club
at www.westvirginiafossilclub.com.

The majority of West Virginia is covered by the Allegheny Plateau. The main range of the Allegheny Mountains runs in a series of rounded parallel ridges though the state from northeast to southwest and east of the Allegheny Escarpment much of the state lies in the valley and ridge province. Clay, sand, gravel, sandstone, limestone and slate predominate, and fossils occur throughout the exposed Silurian, Devonian and Mississippian formations. Fossil coral, petrified wood, chert, agate, and jaspers have been found in Greenbrier, Hampshire, Hardy, Kanawha, Mineral, Monongalia, Monroe, and Pocahontas counties.

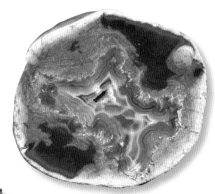

▲ Agate in concretion nodule, West Virginia, **$40**. Jeff Anderson Collection

▲ Rough exterior of Locust Creek petrified coral. Patti Polk image, Jason Badgley Collection

◄ Polished petrified coral, Locust Creek, Pocahontas County, 5" x 2" x 1.5", **$45**.
Patti Polk image,
Jason Badgley Collection

Wisconsin

For more information about rockhounding,
visit the Wisconsin Geological Society at
www.wisgeologicalsociety.com.

Bordered by rivers and lakes, Wisconsin lies on a foundation of Precambrian gneisses, granites, syenites and crystalline rocks. Topographically, Wisconsin was formed by the advance and retreat of all four periods of glaciation during the Pleistocene epoch. The oldest rocks are Eozoic in age, outcropping immediately south of Lake Superior, while a broad exposure of Upper Cambrian crystalline rocks occur throughout the west-central counties. Ordovician formations from a crescent shaped belt extending from Green Bay in Brown County to the Illinois border and north to St. Croix County. Silurian exposures extend all along the eastern part of the state, fronting onto Lake Michigan, while a very narrow strip of Devonian rocks occur between Sheboygan and Milwaukee. Low, rounded hills of the Keweenaw and Gogebic ranges stretch across the northern counties. Lake Superior agates occur in practically every county in almost every gravel deposit or pit, streambed, excavation, mine, or quarry in the state, so they won't be listed individually here. Agatized coral occurs in Rock County in gravel quarries near Afton.

▶ Typical red Lake Superior
banded agate from river gravels,
1.5" x 1" x 1.5", **$15 per pound**.
Patti Polk Collection

◀ Water-worn Lake Superior
banded agate from river
gravels, 1.25" x .75" x 1.5",
$15 per pound. Patti Polk Collection

▶ Gray-colored Lake Superior
banded agate from river gravels,
1" x .75" x 1", **$15 per pound**.
Patti Polk Collection

Wisconsin

Wyoming

For more information about minerals, rocks, fossils, and gemstones, as well as an introduction to the people and places where rockhounds can go, visit the Wyoming State Mineral and Gem Society at wymineralandgemsociety.org.

From barren sagebrush-covered deserts to high plateaus and tall mountain ranges, Wyoming lies at the western end of the Great Plains. From the South Dakota border, the Black Hills travel westward into eroded badlands and sagebrush plains that continue out to the Powder River. Near the middle of the state the Great Plains end abruptly at the foot of the Big Horn Mountains. Stretching south from the Montana line, this mammoth fault block range divides the northern half of the state and terminates in Cloud Peak on the eastern edge of Big Horn County. The tablelands of southeastern Wyoming are interrupted by the mountainous Laramie and Medicine Bow ranges, while western Wyoming is mostly high, rugged mountains that support the great Continental Divide. Both east and west of the Continental Divide lie great areas of opalized and silicified wood, and many areas within the state afford a wide variety of agates, jaspers, and fossils for the collector. Albany, Big Horn, Carbon, Converse, Fremont, Johnson, Lincoln, Natrona, Park, Platte, Sweetwater, Teton, Unita, and Washakie are some of the counties where these materials can be found.

▲ Petrified wood limb in matrix specimen, Eden Valley, Sweetwater County, 3.5" x 3" x 5", **$35**. Patti Polk Collection

▲ Polished petrified wood limb, Eden Valley, Sweetwater County, 4" x 4" x 6", **$40**. Patti Polk Collection

Wyoming

▲ Blue Forest petrified wood limb cast, Eden Valley, Sweetwater County, 1.5" x 1.25" x 3", **$4 per pound**. Patti Polk Collection

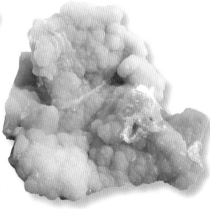

▲ "Youngite," a brecciated jasp-agate typically coated with a fine druzy quartz, Guernsey, Platte County, 3.5" x 3" x 3", **$32 per pound**. Patti Polk image, Jason Badgley Collection

▶ Rough "Youngite" showing druzy quartz coating, Guernsey, Platte County, 3" x 3" x 2", **$35**. Patti Polk Collection

▶ Plume agate slab, Medicine Bow, Carbon County, 5.5" x 4" x .25", **$40**. Patti Polk Collection

◀ Rough plume agate from Medicine Bow, Carbon County, 4" x 2" x 2", **$50**.
Patti Polk Collection

▲ Exterior of a rough piece of oolitic agate, 8.5" x 1.5" x 3".
Patti Polk Collection

▶ Cut face of oolitic agate showing distinct oolites, Tipton, Sweetwater County, 3" x 2.25" x 2", **$25**.
Patti Polk image, Jason Badgley Collection

▲ Old stock pink chalcedony limb cast, Wiggins Fork, Fremont County, 2.75" x 2.5" x 8.5", **$65**. Patti Polk Collection

◄ Rough agatized palm section, Green River Formation, Sweetwater County, 3" x 1.5" x 4", **$9 per pound**. Patti Polk image, Doris Banks Collection

▶ Polished petrified palm specimen, Green River Formation, Sweetwater County, 1.75" x 1" x 2", **$15**. Patti Polk Collection

◄ Rough Dryhead fortification agate, Big Horn Basin, Big Horn County, 3" x 2" x 3", **$45**. Patti Polk Collection

Wyoming

▶ Exterior of Shirley Basin banded jasper.
Patti Polk image, Doris Banks Collection

▲ Cut face of rough banded jasper, Shirley
Basin, Carbon County, 6" x 3.5" x 2", **$20**.
Patti Polk image, Doris Banks Collection

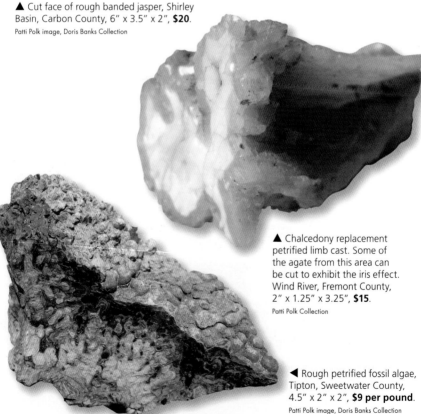

▲ Chalcedony replacement
petrified limb cast. Some of
the agate from this area can
be cut to exhibit the iris effect.
Wind River, Fremont County,
2" x 1.25" x 3.25", **$15**.
Patti Polk Collection

◀ Rough petrified fossil algae,
Tipton, Sweetwater County,
4.5" x 2" x 2", **$9 per pound**.
Patti Polk image, Doris Banks Collection

▼ Opalized petrified wood, Dubois, Fremont County, 4" x 2" x 1.5", **$8 per pound**. Patti Polk image, Doris Banks Collection

◄ Unusual light green, water-worn opalized wood, Fremont County, 3" x 2.5" x 2", **$60**. Patti Polk Collection

▶ "Snakeskin" agate, named for its surface similarity to snakeskin, Jeffrey City, Fremont County, 1" x 1" x .75", **$5**. Patti Polk Collection

Wyoming

◀ Rough Lysite agate with calcite covered botryoidal surfaces, Lysite, Fremont County, 5" x 3.5" x 3", **$10 per pound**.
Patti Polk Collection

▶ Tumbled dendritic moss Sweetwater agate, Jeffrey City, Fremont County, 1" x 1" x .5", **$3**.
Patti Polk Collection

▲ Rough Turitella fossil shell agate, Tipton, Sweetwater County, 5" x 2" x 3", **$14 per pound**.
Patti Polk Collection

Canada

For more information about gems and minerals, visit the Gem & Mineral Federation of Canada at www.gmfc.ca.

Due to its great size and varied geology, I will give a broad overview of the general geology of Canada, but the focus of this section is mainly on the provinces in Canada that have the greatest deposits of agate and jasper, mainly Alberta, British Columbia, Manitoba, Nova Scotia, Ontario, and Quebec.

Canada is geologically one of the oldest countries in the world, and more than half of it consists of Precambrian rocks, which have been above the sea ever since the beginning of the Paleozoic era. The Canadian Shield is a physiographic division, consisting of five smaller physiographic provinces, known as the Laurentian Upland, Kazan Region, Davis, Hudson, and James. The Canadian Shield formed the geologic center around which the North American continent has been built from that time to the present, and also provided the later rocks that were deposited in the shallow seas around its margins. The Precambrian strata of Canada is not evenly distributed, since the western side of the country consists almost wholly of later rocks, while the great peninsula of Labrador on the east belongs wholly to the Archaean series. The later divisions of the Precambrian cover much less land area than the early barren granite and gneiss.

Nearly the whole of the country has been covered with ice sheets within the last million years, and this has happened a number of times, with the result being that a very ancient land surface that had been buried under the ancient debris has been completely remodeled by weathering during the ages. Three vast ice sheets accomplished the work: the Cordilleran sheet, which covered British Columbia and reached the islands along the coast; the Keewatin sheet, which blotted out the whole of the Great Plains; and the Labrador sheet, which covered all of the east except one or two fringe mountain ranges. Almost everywhere in Canada, the effects of these tremendous events are in evidence. The province of Manitoba has many gravel quarries and pits near Souris, where glacially deposited Montana-type moss agates may be recovered.

The Keweenawan sandstones, shales, and great sheets of diabase give rise to basaltic hills and low mountains north of Lake Superior, especially near Thunder Bay in Ontario. Thunder Bay, Michipicoten Island, and Quebec Harbor in Lake Superior all offer fine agate collecting opportunities. Dipping southwestward from the ancient shield in southern Quebec and Ontario, there are Palaeozoic sandstones, limestones, and shales of Ordovician, Silurian, and Devonian age, laid down in a shallow sea and often containing trilobites, brachiopods, and other fossils. The Carboniferous and Permian periods of the later Palaeozoic cover much of the Maritime provinces, as evidenced in regions of New Brunswick and Nova Scotia near the Bay of Fundy. The Fundy Basin is a sediment-filled rift basin on the Atlantic coast of southeastern Canada. It contains three sub-basins; the Fundy sub-basin, the Minas Basin and the Chignecto Basin. These arms meet at the Bay of Fundy, which is contained within the rift valley. The Bay of Fundy in Nova Scotia is a region long recognized as a well-established agate collecting area, especially near Cape Blomidon and Scots Bay, due to the intrusive Triassic basalt layers that occur there.

The Mesozoic era makes up almost the whole of the Great Plains southwest of the Precambrian nucleus of the continent. The latest division of the Mesozoic, the Cretaceous, and its sediments, underlie most of the typical prairie region of the west. Most of the

Cretaceous beds are of land or fresh water origin, and many areas contain fossil remains.

After the Cretaceous beds were formed at, or near sea level, the Rocky Mountains were elevated, and vast amounts of sediments were pushed into great folds or split into long blocks which were tilted and driven upon one another, forming the barren cliffs which give the chain it's name and which rise so abruptly from the flatlands of the prairie.

West of the Rockies are the Selkirk and Gold ranges, older and not quite as high in stature. Next, we come to the interior tableland of British Columbia, cut by valleys and canyons and where fine agates occur near the Monte Lake area, Kamloops, and near Prince George in the river gravels. Unusual thundereggs occur at Black Dome Mountain near Clinton. Finally comes the Coast range of mountains, formed in Jurassic times by the upwelling of molten rock, much like the Laurentian of eastern Canada. These three mountain chains make up most of British Columbia, but still farther to the west rises another discontinuous range in the great island of Vancouver and the smaller Queen Charlotte Islands, where agates may be found along the beaches.

Alberta

The Alberta Federation of Rock Clubs has seven clubs throughout the province. For more information, visit www.afrc.ca.

▲ Water-worn jasper, Bow River, Calgary, 2.5" x 1" x 1", **$2**. Patti Polk image, Doris Banks Collection

British Colombia

The British Columbia Lapidary Society is the umbrella association for rockhounding clubs in the province. For more information, visit www.lapidary.bc.ca.

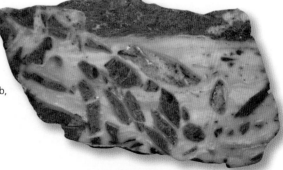

▶ Polished brecciated jasper slab, 6.5" x 3" x .25", **$25**.
Patti Polk Collection

◀ Small beach agate, Agate beach, Queen Charlotte Islands, 1" x .75" x .5", **$2**. Patti Polk Collection

▲ Eye agate, Monte Lake, Kamloops, **$20**. Patti Polk image, Pat McMahan Collection

▲ Eye agate, Monte Lake, Kamloops, **$25**. Patti Polk image, Pat McMahan Collection

◀ Petrified bog, Chilko Lake, 5" x 4" x 4", **$35**. Patti Polk image, Doris Banks Collection

British Colombia

Canada | **237**

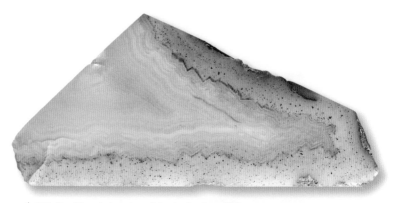

▲ "Disdero" banded agate polished cabochon, **$35**. Lowell Foster Collection

▲ Sagenite agate, Cache Creek, **$45**.
Patti Polk image, Pat McMahan Collection

▶ Agate nodule, Monte Lake,
Kamloops, 1.75" x 1.25" x .5",
$10. Patti Polk Collection

◀ Sagenite agate, Grand Forks, **$40**. Patti Polk image, Pat McMahan Collection

▲ Sagenite agate, Monte Lake, Kamloops, **$45**. Patti Polk image, Pat McMahan Collection

Manitoba

The Mineral Society of Manitoba promotes the study of minerals, rocks and fossils for their scientific and recreational value. For more information, visit www.umanitoba.ca/faculties/science/geological_sciences/mineralsociety/events.html.

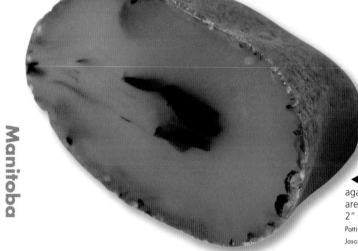

◄ Cut and polished agate from the Souris area gravel pit, 2" x 1" x 1.5", **$3**.
Patti Polk image,
Jason Badgley Collection

► Exterior of a water-worn agate from the Souris area gravel pit, 3" x 1.5" x 2", **$3**. Patti Polk Collection

Nova Scotia

To connect with other people in the hobby in Nova Scotia, visit The Nova Scotia Mineral and Gem Society at nsmgs.ca.

▲ Plume agate from Scots Bay, **$35**. Patti Polk image, Pat McMahan Collection

▲ Cycad limb cast from Ross Creek, 6" x 6" x 9", **$25**. Lance Shope Collection

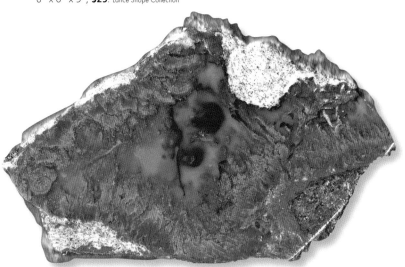

▲ Flame agate specimen from Bay of Fundy, **$60**. Jim Puckett Collection

▲ Group of rare spiral jaspers from Horseshoe Cove, approximately .5" to 1" each, **$10-$15 each**.
Lance Shope Collection

▲ Seam agate from Parrsboro, 2" x .75" x .5", **$20**. Lance Shope Collection

▲ An agate-bearing seam in Ross Creek. Lance Shope Collection

▶ Petrified cycad wood, Ross Creek,
3" x 3" x 2", **$35**. Lance Shope Collection

◀ Flame agate from Horseshoe
Cove, 2" x .75" x 2". **$25**.
Lance Shope Collection

▶ Rough jasp-agate, Cape
Blomidon, 2" x 1.75" x .75",
$25. Lance Shope Collection

▲ Polished flame agate, Bay of Fundy, 6.25" x 2" x 1.25", **$45**. Patti Polk image, Jason Badgley Collection

▶ Banded beach agate, Little Split Cove, 2" x 2" x 1.5", **$3**. Patti Polk Collection

▼ Polished end cut seam jasper, Parrsboro, 1.5" x 1" x .75", **$20**. Lance Shope Collection

▲ Sagenite agate from Scots Bay, **$45**. Patti Polk image, Pat McMahan Collection

▲ Polished petrified wood, Ross Creek, 2" x 2" x 1.5", **$30**. Lance Shope Collection

Ontario

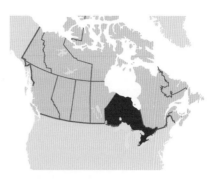

For more information about rockhounding in Ontario, visit the Kingston Lapidary and Mineral Club at www.mineralclub.ca.

Ontario

▲ Banded Lake Superior-type agate from Michipicoten Island, **$35**. Jeff Anderson Collection

► Lacy agate with quartz pockets from Thunder Bay, **$40**. Jeff Anderson Collection

Quebec

The Montreal Gem and Mineral Club serves the gem and mineral hobbyists in Quebec. For more information, visit www. montrealgemmineralclub.ca.

▲ Polished white and coral-colored banded thunderegg from Mont Lyall, Sainte-Anne-des-Monts, **$45**. Jeff Anderson Collection

Mexico

To learn more about the minerals found in Mexico, visit www.galleries.com/minerals/fablocal/mexico.htm.

Northern Mexico can be divided into four physiographic areas. From east to west, these areas are the Basin and Range of eastern Chihuahua, the Sierra Madre Occidental lying along the Chihuahua/Sonora-Sinaloa border, the Parallel Ranges and Valleys, and the Coastal Plain of western Sonora and Sinaloa. The ages of the rocks from these areas range from Precambrian through recent with the most common rock type at the surface being Cenozoic volcanics.

The Basin and Range province (Cuencas y Sierras) ranges from eastern Chihuahua northward through the Trans-Pecos of west Texas and then westward across southern New Mexico into Arizona. The province consists of a series of northwest trending mountain ranges created by the tilting and uplift of Tertiary igneous rocks and/or Mesozoic sediments. These sediments are mainly early Cretaceous limestone, shales, and sandstones with occasional exposures of Paleozoic marine rocks. West of Chihuahua the province is referred to as Altas Llanuras since each valley is progressively higher. La Junta lies near the boundary of the Basin and Range and the Sierra Madre Occidental provinces. The Sierra Madre Occidental is the largest physiographic province in Mexico and contains volcanic terrain starting near the US-Mexico border that trends southeast into the states of Zacatecas and Jalisco. Cenozoic volcanic rocks, mostly tilting to the east, characterize this province. These rocks can be divided into two basic groups, a lower andesitic unit and an upper rhyolitic unit.

The Parallel Ranges and Valleys Province is similar in structural style to the Basin and Range to the east. This province contains Mexico's oldest rocks, the Precambrian intrusives of northwestern Sonora. Younger Precambrian rocks in the Parallel Ranges and Valleys Province include dolomite, limestone, sandstone, and shale. The Coastal Plain is a geographic province between San Blas and Topolobampo, characterized by a relatively flat section of Tertiary and Quaternary gravels and alluvium. In a few places, the flat plain is marked by low hills of basaltic breccia and intrusive volcanics.

For our purposes, we are concerned mainly with the richest agate and jasper bearing states, which include Chihuahua, Coahuila, Durango, Nayarit, Sonora, and Zacatecas. The northern region of Mexico has the greatest concentration of collectible agates and jaspers, primarily found as isolated deposits, mostly within andesites, rhyolites, and ash flow tuffs located on privately owned ranches. Usually, each particular type of agate gets its name from the ranch or nearby landmark where it is mined. In the state of Chihuahua alone, there are many famously recognized agates such as Moctezuma, Coyamito, Agua Nueva, and Laguna, to name just a few. There are so many large and small agate locations scattered throughout northern and central Mexico that whole books have been written on the subject, so only the basics will be covered here.

Unfortunately one cannot simply walk onto a ranch and begin collecting agate. Mexican mining law establishes that all minerals (including agate) found in the Mexican territory are owned by the nation and that private parties may exploit the minerals (except oil, gas, and radioactive minerals) through a concession granted by the federal government. Exploration concessions are initially granted for a period of six years; an exploitation concession for 50 years. Concessions may only be granted to Mexican individuals, ejidos (government communal lands), or companies incorporated pursuant to Mexican law. While a mining concession gives its holder the right to carry out mining work and take ownership of any minerals found, it does not automatically grant any surface access rights, which must be negotiated separately with the owner of the land surface. There are also maintenance obligations that arise from a mining concession to avoid its cancellation, including performance of assessment work, payment of mining taxes, and compliance with environmental laws. While formal claims did not initially exist on the agate deposits, concessions were later granted and remain on all known deposits today.

While the average collector may have difficulty distinguishing between the various types of Mexican agate, each variety of agate has its own specific characteristics that provide them with their own special identity. Unique characteristics such as a specific range of color inclusions, fineness of banding, nodule shape and size, and external features such as pitting and exterior color are clues that help the collector identify the variety and exact location of origin.

Chihuahua

In the state of Chihuahua, there are many famously recognized agates, including Moctezuma, Coyamito, Agua Nueva, and Laguna.

◄ Rough Agua Nueva agate showing pink tubes, 3" x 2" x 3", **$15 per pound**. Patti Polk Collection

◄ Agua Nueva fortification agate with tubes and moss, 2" x 2" x .25", **$20**. Patti Polk Collection

▶ Flame agate showing rough back side.
Patti Polk Collection

▶ Flame agate end cut front side, 4.5″ x 3.5″ x .5″, **$20 per pound**.
Patti Polk Collection

▲ Polished San Carlos sagenite agate, 3″ x 1.5″ x 2″, **$6 per pound**. Patti Polk image, Jason Badgley Collection

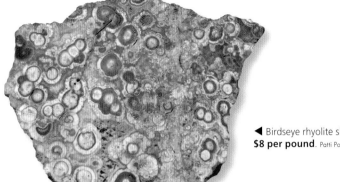

◀ Birdseye rhyolite slab, 4″ x 3″ x .25″, **$8 per pound**. Patti Polk Collection

▲ Mossy Cathedral agate showing botryoidal surface, 4.5″ x 1.5″ x 4″, **$15 per pound**. Patti Polk image, Jason Badgley Collection

▲ Polished Purple Passion slab, 4″ x 2″ x .25″, **$75**. Patti Polk Collection

▶ Polished Laguna agate slab with fortification, **$50**. Patti Polk Collection

▶ Pink and red fortification Laguna agate polished slab with parallax, 3" x 2.5" x .25", **$50**. Patti Polk Collection

▲ Multi-color polished fortification Laguna agate slab, 4" x 2" x .25", **$60**. Patti Polk Collection

◀ Fantasy Jasper slab with ovoid patterns, 4″ x 3″ x .25″, **$15**. Patti Polk Collection

▶ Rough Calandria banded agate, 2.5″ x 1.5″ x 3″, **$8 per pound**. Patti Polk Collection

▲ Crazy Lace agate slab, 5″ x 2″ x .25″, **$10 per pound**. Patti Polk Collection

▶ Rough Parselas banded agate, 2" x 1" x 1.5", **$28 per pound**.
Patti Polk Collection

◀ Polished Parselas agate cabochon by the author, 30mm x 20mm, **$40**.
Patti Polk Collection

▶ Cut El Sueco agate with moss, 2" x 1.25" x 2", **$18**.
Patti Polk Collection

◀ Polished half geode with crystals in center,
3″ x 3″ x 2″, **$9 per pound**. Patti Polk Collection

◀ Falling Star rhyolite
slab, 4″ x 3″ .25″,
$4 per pound.
Patti Polk image,
Jason Badgley Collection

▶ Moctezuma polished half
nodule, 2″ x 1.5″ x 2″, **$50**.
Patti Polk Collection

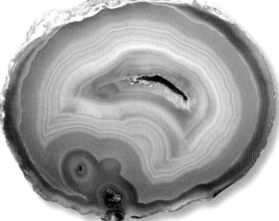

▶ Calico Lace slab, 4" x 4" x .25", **$18**. Patti Polk Collection

◀ Polished Carneros banded and moss agate nodule, 3" x 3" x 2", **$45**.
Patti Polk image, Jason Badgley Collection

▶ Polished "Red Hot" Barrendo thunderegg, 2" x 1.5" x 1", **$10 per pound**.
Patti Polk image, Jason Badgley Collection

Chihuahua

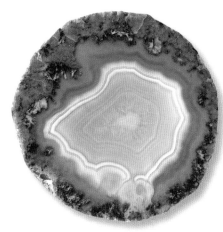

◀ Polished Las Choyas agate-filled coconut with center floater and banding, 3″ x 3″ x 2″, **$8 per pound**.
Patti Polk Collection

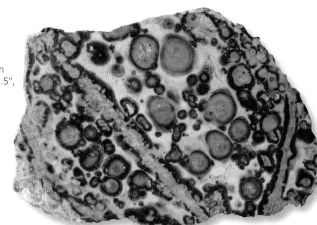

▶ Rough Leopardskin rhyolite, 2.5″ x 2″ x 1.5″, **$8 per pound**.
Patti Polk image,
Jason Badgley Collection

◀ Rosetta Lace agate slab, 5″ x 4″ x .25″, **$10 per pound**. Patti Polk Collection

▶ Polished Rivera plume slab,
4″ x 3″ x .25″, **$45**. Patti Polk image,
Jason Badgley Collection

▶ Casas Grande
polished nodule,
2.5″ x 2″ x 2″, **$35**.
Patti Polk Collection

◀ Coyamito polished half
nodule, 1.5″ x 1″ x .75″,
$90. Patti Polk Collection

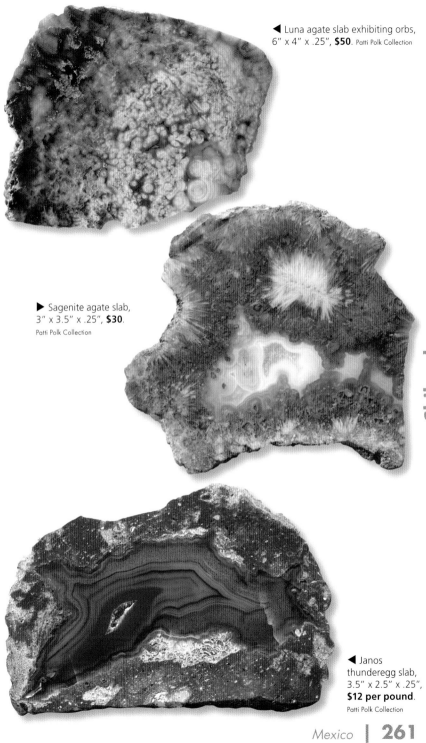

◀ Luna agate slab exhibiting orbs, 6" x 4" x .25", **$50**. Patti Polk Collection

▶ Sagenite agate slab, 3" x 3.5" x .25", **$30**.
Patti Polk Collection

◀ Janos thunderegg slab, 3.5" x 2.5" x .25", **$12 per pound**.
Patti Polk Collection

Chihuahua

Coahuila

In additon to agates, a variety of prized grossular, known as "raspberry garnet," is found in Coahuila.

▲ Agatized fossil stromatolite, Cuatro Cienegas, 2.5" x 1.5" x 1.5", **$40**.
Patti Polk image, Jason Badgley Collection

Durango

Besides agates and jaspers, Durango's
Mapimi has fluorescent adamite,
as well as hemimorphite and wulfenite.

▲ Royal Aztec polished specimen, 3" x 2" x 2", **$60**. Patti Polk image, Jason Badgley Collection

Durango

Nayarit

Nayarit is one of the richest agate and jasper bearing states in Mexico.

▲ Slab of Parrot Wing jasper, a jasper that is included with chrysocolla and cuprite, 3" x 1.5" x .25", **$12 per pound**. Patti Polk Collection

Sonora

The ages of rocks from the Sonora area range from Precambrian through recent, with the most common rock type at the surface being Cenozoic volcanics.

◀ Rough chunk of porcelain jasper, 6" x 5" x 3", **$6 per pound**. Patti Polk Collection

▲ Rough cut "Sonoran Sunset," a chalcedony included with cuprite, 2" x 1" x 1", **$20 per pound**. Patti Polk Collection

▲ "Sonora Dendritic" rhyolite slab, 5" x 2.5" x .25", **$12 per pound**. Patti Polk Collection

▲ Polished agate specimen with banding and sagenite inclusions, **$80**. Patti Polk image, Pat McMahan Collection

Zacatecas

Zacatecas is one of the localities within Mexico well known for its collection of mineral specimens.

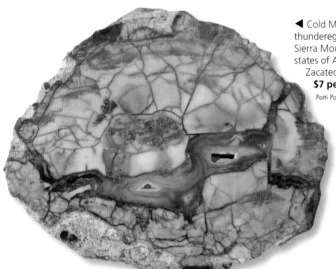

◀ Cold Mountain thunдеregg, mined in the Sierra Mountains between the states of Aguascalientes and Zacatecas, 3.5" x 3" x 2.5", **$7 per pound**.
Patti Polk Collection

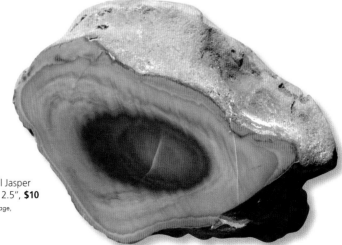

▶ Rough cut Imperial Jasper nodule, 3.5 x 2.25" x 2.5", **$10 per pound**. Patti Polk image, Jason Badgley Collection

▲ Cut geode showing druzy quartz crystals in center void with wispy cloud patterns in chalcedony, 3" x 2.5" x 2", **$8 per pound**. Patti Polk image, Jason Badgley Collection

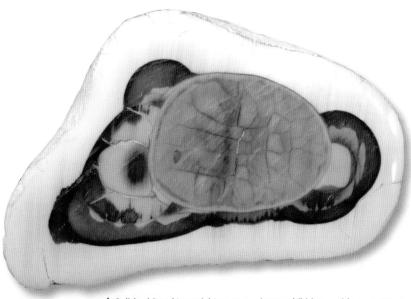

▲ Polished Royal Imperial Jasper specimen exhibiting ovoid egg patterns, **$80**. Patti Polk image, Pat McMahan Collection

Resources

CONTRIBUTORS WEBSITES

www.achate.at (Johann Zenz collectible agate website)
www.agatecollectorsdream.com (Grant Curtis collectible agate website)
www.agatecreek.com.au/ (Darren Jones Australian collectible agate website)
www.agategrrrl.com (Patti Polk collectible agate website)
www.agateshowcase.com (Jim Puckett collectible agate website)
www.agateswithinclusions.com (Pat McMahan collectible agate website)
www.californiaagategallery.com (Jason Badgley collectible agate website)
www.jimbanks.com (Jim Banks fine photography website)
www.mainelyagates.com (Lance Shope collectible agate website)
www.mcrocks.com (Mike Streeter collectible agate, jasper, & minerals website)
www.ramseyssedona.com (Jeff Goebel rock and jewelry shop)
www.sailorenergy.net/Minerals/MineralMain.html (Jeff Anderson collectible agate website)
www.shininglightstudios.com (Custom made stained glass arts by Greg Rosenberg)
www.ssrockshop.com (Spanish Stirrup Rock Shop)
www.sterlinghillminingmuseum.org (Richard Hauck, Sterling Hill Mining Museum)
www.worldofjaspers.com (Hans Gamma collectible jaspers website)

RECOMMENDED READING

Agates I, II & III by Johann Zenz
Agate Hunting Made Easy by Jim Magnuson
Agates Inside Out by Karen Brzys
Ancient Forests: A Closer Look at Fossil Wood by Frank J. Daniels & Richard D. Dayvault
A Rockhounding Guide to North Carolina's Blue Ridge Mountains by Michael Streeter
Coast to Coast Gem Atlas by Johnson & Johnson (field collecting guide)
Collecting Rocks, Gems, & Minerals by Patti Polk
Dictionary of Geological Terms by the American Geological Institute
Dryhead Agate by John Hurst
Earth Treasures Volumes 1-4 by Allan Eckert (field collecting guides)
Fairburn Agate by Roger Clark
Fee Mining & Mineral Adventures in the Eastern U.S. by James & Jeanette Monaco
Fee Mining & Rockhounding Adventures in the West by James & Jeanette Monaco
Field Collecting Gemstones & Minerals by John Sinkankas
Flintknapping - Making and Understanding Stone Tools by John C. Whittaker
Geodes - Nature's Treasures by Brad Cross & June Culp Zeitner
Geological Society of America publications (www.geology.gsapubs.org)
Geology Underfoot and Roadside Geology book series (geology by state or region, available at www.geology.com/store/roadside-geology.shtml)
Gemstones of North America by John Sinkankas
Gem Trail Guide Series (collecting locations by state)
Lake Superior Rocks & Minerals by Bob Lynch & Dan Lynch
Petrified Wood: The World of Fossilized Wood, Cones, Ferns, and Cycads by Frank J. Daniels
Picture Jaspers - Treasures of the Owyhee area, Oregon by Hans Gamma

Prospecting for Gemstones and Minerals by John Sinkankas
Rock & Gem Magazine (www.rockngem.com)
The Beauty of Banded Agates by Michael Carlson
The Book of Agates by Lelande Quick
The Lake Superior Agate by Scott Wolter
The Other Lake Superior Agates by John D. Marshall
The Practical Geologist by Dougal Dixon
The Rockhound's Handbook by James Mitchell

TOPOGRAPHIC MAPS & GPS SUPPLIES

www.garmin.com
www.gpscity.com
www.usgs.gov/pubprod/maps.html

GEM & MINERAL SHOWS, DEALERS

Martin Zinn Expositions (www.mzexpos.com)
Quartzsite PowWow Gem & Mineral Show (www.qiaaz.org)
Tucson Gem & Mineral Show (www.tgms.org or www.jewelryshowguide.com)
Rimrock Gems, Halfway, OR (541) 742-4608
www.AgateNodule.com
www.RareRocksandGems.com
www.TheGemShop.com

GEM & MINERAL ORGANIZATIONS/CLUBS

American Federation of Mineralogical Societies (www.amfed.org)
Gem and Mineral Federation of Canada (www.gmfc.ca)
Geological Society of America (www.geosociety.org)

EARTH SCIENCE & NATURAL HISTORY MUSEUMS

Arizona-Sonora Desert Museum (www.desertmuseum.org)
Kuban's Guide to Natural History Museums in the U.S.
    (www.paleo.cc/kpaleo/museums.htm#us)
Lizzardo Museum of Lapidary Art (www.lizzardomuseum.org)
Rice Northwest Museum (www.ricenorthwestmuseum.org)
Smithsonian Museum of Natural History Mineral Sciences Collections
    (www.mineralsciences.si.edu/collections.htm)

GENERAL INTEREST & FRIENDS ON FACEBOOK

Agategrrrl/Patti Polk: www.facebook.com/pages/Agategrrrl
Jason Badgley: www.facebook.com/jason.badgley
Charles Bennett: www.facebook.com/charles.bennett
Mark Berreth: www.facebook.com/mark.berreth
Warren Bobyk: www.facebook.com/warren.bobyk
DB's Agates: www.facebook.com/dbs.agates
Barbara Grill: www.facebook.com/barbara.grill
Bruce Nedwich: www.facebook.com/bruce.nedwich
John D. Marshall: www.facebook.com/john.d.marshall.5

Bibliography

American Geological Institute, *Dictionary of Geological Terms*;
    Dolphin Books, 1962.

Dake, H. C. & Fleener, F. & Wilson, B. H.; *Quartz Family Minerals*;
    McGraw-Hill, 1938.

Eckhert, Allan, *Earth Treasures Volumes 1-4*; Backinprint.com.

Emmons, C. & Fenton, M., *Geology Principles and Processes*; McGraw-Hill, 1955.

Gamma, H., *Picture Jaspers - Treasures of the Owyhee Area, Oregon*;
    Paper Chase Press, 2011.

Leiper, H., *Agates of North America*; Lapidary Journal, 1966.

MacFall, Russell, *Gem Hunter's Guide*; Thomas Y. Crowell Co., 1975.

Pabian, Roger & Brian Jackson; *Agates, Treasures of the Earth*, Firefly Books, 2009.

Polk, Patti, *Collecting Rocks, Gems, & Minerals*; Krause Publications, 2012.

Pearl, R. M., *Successful Mineral Collecting & Prospecting*; Bonanza Books, 1961.

Quick, L., *The Book of Agates*; Chilton Books, 1963.

Ransom, J., *Gems and Minerals of America*; Harper & Row, 1975.

Sinkankas, J., *Prospecting for Gemstones and Minerals*;
    Van Nostrand Reinhold Co., 1970.

Sinkankas, J., *Gemstones & Minerals*; D, Van Nostrand Co., 1961.

Zeitner, J. C., *Gem & Lapidary Materials*; Geoscience Press, 1996.

Zenz, J., *Agates I, II, & III*; Bode Publishing, 2005, 2009, 2011.

State-by-state field collecting guidebooks.

www.snr.unl.edu/data/geologysoils/agates/index-agates.asp
    (University of Nebraska agate database website).